The Way of the Tao
Living an Authentic Life

Lao Tzu's Tao Te Ching
A Treatise and Interpretation
By
Dennis M Waller

Edited by Sherry Thoman

Copyright © 2012 Dennis M Waller

All rights reserved.

ISBN:1475268882
ISBN-13: 978-1475268881

DEDICATION

Thank you Doan Pham for your support

Tại sao tôi không thể nói khi tôi có rất nhiều để cho biết? Tại sao tôi không thể viết khi tôi có rất nhiều trong tâm trí? Tại sao tôi không thể hát khi có âm nhạc trong trái tim của tôi? Tại sao tôi không thể nhảy khi có nhịp điệu trong không khí? Quá nhiều từ trái ngầm. Quá nhiều thứ để lại hoàn tác. Tại sao nó không thể và tại sao có thể không tôi? Cho tất cả tôi biết sâu trong cơn đau này. Lấy sự vui vẻ từ trái tim của tôi. Đây có phải là những đau đớn của thiếu bạn? Đây có phải là lý do đằng sau tất cả? Nghe các khổ của trái tim tôi. Khao cho bạn và cho liên lạc của bạn. Cảm giác môi của bạn, cảm thấy khuôn mặt của bạn. Thiếu hôn và ôm hôn nồng nhiệt của bạn. Khi chờ đợi bao giờ sẽ hơn? Cho miễn là được ngoài tôi có thể không bao giờ được toàn bộ. Tình yêu của tôi. Tôi chỉ muốn bạn biết. Rằng trái tim của tôi đau vì tôi là thiếu bạn.

CONTENTS

PREFACE — i

FOREWORD — v

INTRODUCTION to LAO TZU — ix

CHAPTER 1 – THE WAY of THE TAO — 1

CHAPTER 2- LIVING an AUTHENTIC LIFE with THE TAO — 11

CHAPTER 3- THE ART of LIVING in ONENESS — 17

CHAPTER 4- THE TAO and THE ART of SURFING — 23

CHAPTER 5- THE ESSENCE of NATURE — 27

CHAPTER 6- A ROSE by any other Name... — 33

CHAPTER 7- JOHN LENNON, IMAGINE, and THE TAO — 45

CHAPTER 8- NATIVE AMERICANS and THE TAO — 51

CHAPTER 9- SINGULARITY in a DUALISTIC WORLD and LANGUAGE — 59

CHAPTER 10- THE DISCONNECTION from NATURE — 65

CHAPTER 11- WHAT does AWAKENING to THE TAO LOOKS LIKE? — 71

CHAPTER 12- THE TAO from a CHRISTIAN PERSPECTIVE — 75

CHAPTER 13- LIVING YOUR PURPOSE — 78

CHAPTER 14- THE TAO TE CHING — 83

Dennis M Waller

PREFACE

Oscar Wilde is quoted as saying,

"Nowadays people know the price of everything and the value of nothing."

Still rings true today. Actually, when you look back throughout history, this statement can be applied to any age. I imagine this was as true for Lao Tzu's time as for any other time. This is the enduring quality about the Tao. The wisdom of the Tao is needed as much today as it was back then. The lesson here is that no matter how much things change, man stays the same. While technology marches on, the issues of man stay the same.

Tony Robbins said he discovered during his research that the same basic problems of humanity exist everywhere. He said it didn't matter what continent, what religion, what race or what belief system people were or held, they all have, for the most part, the same basic problems and issues.

He also said that there are only about twelve universal problems related to people and their relationships throughout the world. This is because we all appear to be very similar in our emotional make-up. This shows that as a species our basic operating system is basically the same throughout the world, it transcends all dogmas, religious or otherwise.

Most of us are so focused on the "price" that we fail to see the "value". The Tao provides a perspective to show us the value. It all depends on what perspective or tool we choose to use to look at life. That perspective will determine if we see the price or the value.

I want to show you what the world looks like through the eyes of people who see the value. Through illustrations throughout the book, you will begin to see what life can be like when you are living the way of the Tao. The way of the Tao can be seen clearly through the eyes of the enlightened ones.

The following passage is from Henri Frederic Amiel, a Swiss philosopher from the 1800's. The way he looked at life is a fair representation of what life looks like when living in the Tao. He was aware not only of the price but of the value. His sense of value is in his appreciation for nature and all living things and an awareness of the innerconnectiveness of life. This passage shows his insight into this principle.

Aix-les-Bains, France, September 7th, 1851 – Henri Frederic Amiel- *"It is ten o'clock at night. A strange and mystic moonlight, with a fresh breeze and a sky crossed by a few wandering clouds, makes our terrace delightful. These pale and gentle rays shed from the zenith a subdued and penetrating peace; it is like the calm joy or the pensive smile of experience, combined with a certain stoic strength. The stars shine, the leaves tremble in the silver light. Not a sound in all the landscape; great gulfs of shadow under the green alleys and at the steps. Everything is secret, solemn, and mysterious.*

O night hours, hours of silence and solitude! With you are grace and melancholy; you sadden and you console. You speak to us of all that has passed away, and of all that must die, but you say to us; Courage while you promise us rest."

Dennis M Waller

FOREWORD

The Tao is much deeper than the paltry 81 verses. It doesn't require any formal instructions or the need to memorize text. It isn't a religion or a dogma. There are no special ceremonies or need of offerings. It is just a simple handbook to life, a guide to understanding life.

All the Tao ask of you is for your willingness to go within yourself to find the answers. Within all of us is the key to the universe. It is the key to unlock all the mysteries of humanity. Within us all are the answers we are seeking. In order to reach that place we need to make a commitment to ourselves and break free from the attachment to our ego, break free from the preconditioning of society and start on the path to rediscovering our authentic self. The Tao can provide that path if you approach it with an open mind and heart.

The Tao is a very short book you can read in one afternoon, but can take a lifetime to master. The Tao isn't a "quick fix" solution; it's more of a lifestyle requiring constant practice. The Tao shows you how to see the value. To understand and appreciate value is to know the meaning of life.

When I set out to do this project it wasn't to be cute or artsy nor was I trying to write in the eloquent style of Herman Melville or Ralph Waldo Emerson. Instead I took the advice of William Faulkner and just wrote. Faulkner said to just write and teach yourself by your mistakes, people learn only by error. In other words, just get out there and do it! Faulkner could have been talking about life too. Just do it! Sound familiar? So, here is my interpretation of the Tao of what it means to me, good, bad or indifferent, it is for you to decide.

I believe man is good and decent at his core; that all individuals, no matter how malevolent they may be, can be brought back to a natural state of love and compassion. It just seems some of us have become lost along the way. The Tao offers a way to find that love and compassion again.

With persistence, intelligence, and compassion, it is possible to bring about a rich and rewarding life, but all change must begin from within. Gandhi once said, "Be the change you seek." The Tao shows you how to bring about the change you desire and stay on the path.

There are over 45 translations of the Tao into English. Translation really isn't the proper word to use; a better word to use is interpretation. When you start reading some of these translations, you'll soon realize that they are as varied as the number of translations. The Tao touches everyone a little different and some people more than just a little. How the Tao affects you will depend on where you are on the path of Life.

A common thread of the Tao is its paradoxical nature. There are several of the verses that might be challenging. I discovered in order to comprehend a paradox; you must first bend your mind around the paradox until you become the paradox itself! I know this statement might not make any sense but in time it will.

There is a repetitive nature to this book. This is by design to afford you with an opportunity to see the principles of the Tao from different perspectives. To truly comprehend a concept, you must look at it from all sides. By seeing all possible perspectives you are able to shed any bias or judgment. The repetitive nature of the book is to remove any "one-sidedness" and to provide ample points of view.

My goal in doing so is to give you plenty of information so you may come to your own educated conclusions or opinions. It doesn't matter if you agree or disagree with my thoughts, what does matter is if I got you to think. If I got you to think then I have accomplished my goal.

Another approach I took was to use seemingly unrelated people and events like Doctor Phil, John Lennon, Ralph Waldo Emerson, Chief Seattle, Marcus Aurelius, George Carlin, Surfing, and World War One. The average person would be hard pressed to see any connection between them. This book will show the connection between these people and events in demonstrating the universal nature of the Tao. By connecting these dots I am able to present the bigger picture of the world that we don't see.

What resonated with me about the Tao is that it transcends all religious dogmas. It doesn't matter what your affiliation might or might not be. Maybe you don't even have an affiliation with any group. This is the beauty of the Tao. It just doesn't matter if you are Jewish, Christian, Buddhism, Muslim, or a Pagan. The principals of the Tao apply to everybody. The Tao isn't based on any one belief system. The teachings of the Tao are universal. This is the key to the Tao surviving throughout the years. It is a simple handbook on how to approach and live life.

INTRODUCTION TO LAO TZU

The Tao Te Ching is attributed to Lao Tzu and is believed to have been written in the 6th century BCE. Lao Tzu was a contemporary of Confucius, with Lao Tzu being his elder by approximately 40 years. Lao Tzu is considered to be the founder of Taoism and Confucius the founder of Confucianism. Around the same time, we had Plato and Socrates in Greece and the Buddha in India. What an interesting time it must have been to have such great masters living at the same time.

There is a huge difference in the doctrines of Confucius and Lao Tzu. Confucius focused on bringing about order to the social and political life of the times, the ethics being admittedly human and relative. Lao Tzu's focus was to become more introspective in finding your inner peace and Oneness with nature, in other words, more divine and absolute. One is the yin while the other is the yang. Confucius knew that one complemented the other like night and day. Confucius had a deep respect and reverence for Lao Tzu.

It is said that Confucius went to meet Lao Tzu. At the time Lao Tzu was in Luoyang, the ancient capital of China. After his meeting with Lao Tzu, Confucius is quoted as saying this about Lao Tzu:

"I know how birds fly, how fishes swim, and how animals run. But the bird can be shot down by an arrow, a fish can be caught in a net and an animal snared in a trap. But there is the dragon: I cannot tell how he mounts on the wind through the clouds, and rises to heaven. Today I have seen Lao Tzu, and can only compare him to the dragon"

Probably the greatest legend surrounding Lao Tzu is how the Tao came into existence. He had been the keeper of the imperial archives in Luoyang and was well known throughout the land for his wisdom. It is said that Lao Tzu had grown tired of the ways of his fellow man and of all the wars and wished to leave Luoyang.

Mounting a water buffalo, he decided to leave town and go to the desert. Upon reaching the city gate, a gatekeeper by the name of Yin Hsi recognized him. He realized by the way Lao Tzu was packed that he was wasn't going to return. The gatekeeper not wanting him to leave convinced Lao Tzu in order to leave the city he must write down the Tao so it could be preserved. Lao Tzu jumped off the water buffalo and hurriedly wrote down the Tao. Once Lao Tzu completed his task he remounted his water buffalo and left, never to be seen or heard from again.

What remains today is a book surrounded in mystery and intrigue just like the author. Who really knows the true story? What does matter is this little book contains wisdom that is unparalleled. The Tao has been translated more than any other book except the Bible. There are over 250 Western translations with over 45 of those in English. The Tao is considered one of the most influential books of wisdom ever written.

CHAPTER ONE

THE WAY OF THE TAO

This chapter will shed some light on some of the principles of the Tao. All that is required is just a slight shift in your way of thinking of who you are and how you choose to see the world. With an open mind, you can begin on the way of the Tao. All it takes is a simple decision to follow it.

What is the Way of the Tao? It is the way things are in their own natural progression of life and death. The way of intelligent design as shown in nature, this is the way of the Tao. It is the way without a way with no dogmas, no formalities or no religion. It is nothing yet it is everything. This is the way of the Tao. In the words of Winston Churchill, the Tao can be described as a riddle wrapped in a mystery inside an enigma. This is true for people who are attached to their identity and their ego. However the way is clear to those who have mastered and tempered their ego.

"Those who speak do not know. Those who know do not speak." - Lao Tzu

This is a very paradoxical statement. If this is the case, then how was Lao Tzu able to recite the Tao? Lao Tzu wasn't trying to define the Tao. Rather he used the Tao to speak through it. This is critical in order to understand the Tao and what Lao Tzu was saying. Knowledge is the act of "knowing" and Wisdom is the act of "being." When you are in a state of "being," you cannot articulate the meaning of that state. The wisdom of the Tao is beyond knowing, it resides in the "being" not in the "doing."

Verse Twenty One from the Tao- *"The greatest virtue is to be one with the Tao. Not by doing but by being, not by striving but by thriving. The Tao is ever elusive and obscure. While vague and elusive it is seeable in its actions..."*

An example of "being" is right above your head. Look at the sky to see this principle at work. Does the sky try to control the clouds or stop the rain? Does it try to capture them and hold them back? Does it force its will upon the clouds? No, the sky allows the clouds to pass by. Whatever comes, even a thunderstorm, the sky allows it to happen for this is the nature of the sky and the nature of the thunderstorm.

The sky is in harmony by allowing things to be what they are. No control, no agenda, just existing in harmony and balance. Even the wind is free to come and go as she likes. The sky provides the emptiness, the space for these things to be. The sky is like the divine consciousness that cannot be seen, it is only through the action of the wind, the clouds, the thunderstorms that the sky can be known. It is known through action. The Tao is the same, made visible by action.

This quote from Cheng-tao Ke shows the concept of verse twenty one by illustrating the sky within the framework of the Tao quite clearly,

"Like the empty sky it has no boundaries, yet it is right in this place, ever profound and clear. When you seek to know it, you cannot see it. You cannot take hold of it, but you cannot lost it. In not being able to get it, you get it. When you are silent, it speaks; when you speak it is silent. The great gate is wide open to bestow alms, and no crowd is blocking the way."

Another example of "being" is to imagine a mirror that reflects reality; it reflects the images without judgment or prejudice. The mirror doesn't create attachments to the imagines nor does it create an identity of itself based on the imagines. The mirror simply reflects what is cast across its surface. The mirror didn't ask for the images nor does it rejects any of the images. It is simply there being a mirror. It doesn't try to hold on to whatever comes its way or does it try to identify with the images. It just reflects the world as it sees it. When you are living in the way of the Tao you merely observe events happening to you without taking the effects of the events personally. You have a knowing that you are not the events. You are like the mirror and just reflecting them.

This is one of the issues of the Tao that is difficult for people to understand. Within the Tao, you are not identified with any of these events. Most people need to identify themselves through their events and their experiences; this is their Ego at work. You must learn to balance your ego with your authentic self before progressing on the path of the Tao.

When your mind is free from the constraints of the ego as well as free from attachments, it functions in the world but isn't influenced by the actions of the world nor is your mind affected by these actions. This is the way of the Tao.

Verse Four of the Tao- *"The Tao is like a vase that is empty yet used. It is the emptiness that gives birth to the vase. This emptiness, deep and unfathomable, is the source of the ten thousand things"*

Another concept of the Tao is living in emptiness. It is within the emptiness where creation is born. Take a look at a vase. If there wasn't for the emptiness inside the vase, there would be no vase. It is the emptiness that makes the vase. It is the same with a room, without a door, how would one gain entrance? Without a window, how could there be light? It is through the empty space that makes the room useful. Or a boat, without the emptiness within the boat, the boat would not be of any use, or worse, sink. This is true throughout the universe, everywhere you look. This is what was meant by, "The usefulness of what is depends on what is not." There is an unlimited supply of emptiness; learn to take advantage of it.

The Tao is also about the art of letting go and letting be. This is known as the practice of non-interference. The practice of non-interference within the Tao is reminiscence of the old nursery rhyme that we were all taught as children, "Row, row, row your boat, gently down the stream, merrily, merrily, merrily, merrily, life is but a dream." It doesn't say to frantically row against the current or to stress out because you wanted to go in a different direction. No, it says go gently down the stream and be merry about it. At the essence of life, at its deepest core, this is a fundamental truth. This is the lesson that we need to master, learning to let go, let be and go with the flow of life.

In order to let go, we must first learn to trust. Trust is a key element, learning to trust nature, to trust our fellow man and most importantly, to trust ourselves. When you have trust in yourself and have a knowing of the true nature of nature, it is easier to let go. Epictetus said that the first rule of life is letting things go and let them run their course. This is the precept of the Tao. Follow nature in her example on how to live life with balance and in harmony.

All we need to do is look at nature to see this application in use. I have never seen an Oak tree trying or wishing to be an Elm tree, or a shrub wanting to move to another part of the yard because that's where the shrubs with all the money live. I have never seen a Mockingbird in a store buying blue dye in order to become a Blue Jay. I have yet to see a chipmunk in therapy because of its lack of success or thinking his problems were due to an absent or abusive mother. No, in nature there is harmony, balance and understanding of the purpose of all living things. In nature we see the harmonic balance of life as it is meant to be. In nature all living things know their purpose and live accordingly.

Knowledge comes from tuition while Wisdom comes from intuition. In order to enter into the realm of wisdom, you must check your ego and intellectual pride. You must become like a new born child. A new born child has no preconceived notions of what society expects or has had time to form opinions based on a belief system that has been forced upon him. It is a virtue to know the difference between knowledge and wisdom and to live free of the good opinion of others. A Sage of the Tao acts in this accordance.

The characteristics observed in a Sage of the Tao are simplicity, humility, self-surrender, self-giving beyond measure, generosity, compassion, equanimity, forgiving, sense of calmness and inner peace, kind, wise, loving, virtuous, ethical, noble, gentle, to serve and enrich humanity, and to live a Christ-like life.

The Sage knows to do the right thing at the right time in the right manner. The Sage is consistent in his attitude, always staying centered and balanced. He is able to maintain his peace because his inner-self resides in peace. The external Tao expressed is a reflection of the Sage's internal state. True wisdom comes from that same internal place. It is shown by the intuitive nature of the Sage. This intuitive nature comes from trusting in oneself. This is an underlying principle of the Tao, trust.

Another concept of the Tao is living in truth. There might not be anything more important than to be true to yourself and live in truth. To live in a state of truth, to be true to your soul is to allow the voice of the divine consciousness to speak to you. The voice you hear is called intuition, it comes through your consciousness. Robert Browning wrote about truth in his work called Paracelsus. Here are his thoughts on truth-

"Truth is within ourselves; it takes no rise from outward things, whatever you may believe. There is an inmost center in us all, where truth abides in fullness."

A basic truth is to know the divine consciousness; this is to know the Tao. Within the divine there is no separation, only unity, this is the Tao. Another basic truth is in order to find the truth you must stop searching for it. Let go of your opinions and judgments. To realize the truth don't be for or against anything. Free yourself of your attachments to your opinions and judgments.

The Tao talks about the strength of yielding in life. An example of this principle is to look at a Palm tree. Having been through two hurricanes I can speak firsthand of their ability to yield. When the devastating winds of a hurricane makes landfall, the Oak and Elm trees snap like twigs. As strong as an Oak is, it is no match for winds in excess of 140 miles an hour. However the lowly Palm tree in the face of a hurricane can bend all the way to the ground. I have seen the tops of these tall trees bent over to the ground and stay there during the onslaught of the devastating winds of a hurricane.

Once the storm was over and the sun returned, the Palm trees return back to their normal stance as if nothing had ever happened. This is the power of yielding. This is the point that the Tao is making. Be like the Palm tree in the face of adversity, defect the onslaught rather than meet it head on, be yielding. During the trials and tribulations of life remember that it is only temporary, that this too will pass.

To live in the Tao is to live in peace and harmony. The Tao gives you the knowledge of being one with the higher realm of divine consciousness and to experience the innerconnectiveness to all living things. It is to have the awareness of being in this world while knowing that you are not part of it because you are more than all of this. You are one and 10,000 things at the same moment. You are the song that the bird sings, the breeze blowing through the trees, the fish swimming in a brook, the warmth of the sun shining from above, the coolness of the earth below your feet, you are life and death, all at once and not at all. There is no separation in Oneness. In the words of Alan Watts, "When you look out of your eyes at nature happening out there, you're looking at you, the real you. The you that goes on of itself." All you see is nothing more than the different facets of the jewel that we call the universe with us being a part of that jewel.

Verse Thirteen of the Tao- *"Meet failure or success with grace, honor and kindness. Accept misfortune or fortune with grace, honor and kindness. Why? Do not be concerned with either. Accept all that comes your way. Good and evil comes from having a body as the cost of being human. Good or evil cannot affect the true essence of the soul for man is eternal..."*

Living in the Tao, you will respond with the same unconditional loving kindness and compassion to whatever comes your way. Now here is the tricky part. With the Tao, you still feel pain and joy. Experiencing emotions is necessary for humans. The difference is with the Tao; you do not react to the negative experiences with revenge or anger. Nor do you repay a derogatory compliment with an equally negative one. With the Tao you learn equanimity.

When you practice equanimity you'll study the negative experience, play with it, ask why, look at it inside out, learn from it and then let it go. All the while you respond with love and compassion. That is the bottom line to the Tao, learning to let go without the need to react. It is creating a state of evenness that is unbiased to the events or people involved. It is an understanding that the experiences and events are nothing more than "just being."

In mastering the way of the Tao, you'll realize that there is no good or evil, only "just being." That everything is in a transience state of change. More importantly, in mastering this principle, you'll know that you are not these events no more than a mirror is the sky just because it reflects the sky. You'll discover by studying these events, you'll develop a deeper meaning and understanding of what these events mean. You'll also see how your reactions to these events affect others. And in the end, you'll learn to let them go.

With the Tao, you'll learn while living in this Dualist World that authentic pain is necessary in order to appreciate authentic joy. You cannot have one without the other. That is a law of our universe; you must have both in order to know one from the other.

To whatever level of authentic pain you'll experience, you'll be able to experience authentic joy to the same level. You cannot know ecstatic states of joy without knowing the abysmal depths of pain. This is the grace of dealing with the darkness of painful events, knowing that you must master these painful emotions in order to master and recognize true authentic joy.

When you can embrace and rejoice in the moments of pain and suffering with a sympathetic joy, respond with an unconditional love and compassion while staying centered in peace, you have learned the way of the Tao.

With the Tao you'll realize that you are from the same divine source as everyone else and we are all part of the same divine creation. We all have a divine perfection within each and every one of us. Even when the other people don't see the divine perfection, you will. You'll see the many faces of God in everyone you meet.

This is one of the lessons of the Tao. It's teaching us that in love or war, in losing or winning, in success or failure, or in life or death, you will not be overcome by ego and allow yourself to fall prey to the negative self-destructive emotions that the ego enjoys so much. Instead you'll keep a tranquil state of mind, a steady evenness and stay centered in peace at all times. You will know that this too will pass. You'll radiate an abundance of loving compassion at all times. When you master this principle, you will have become a Taoist Sage living in the great way of the Tao.

CHAPTER TWO

LIVING AN AUTHENTIC LIFE WITH THE TAO

"The Authentic self is the soul made visible" – Sarah Ban Breathnach

The Tao is an ancient philosophy of living by the laws of the natural world. It shows the way of how to get back to being your Authentic Self, your Spiritual Self. The Tao has the power to help you reclaim your life from the temporal ego identity that is imprisoning you. With the Tao you can discover your Authentic Identity by getting back to the being-ness and oneness of living in the Divine Consciousness. Through discovering these truths we can become the co-creators of the universe instead of the passive observers we have been. We can learn to live life in the infinity of the moment verses living in the clutches of the Ego. The Tao shows us how to grow detached from the ego identity by becoming in direct contact with our true intent and motives that was meant for us. When we do, we begin to see ourselves as we truly are. It is through being authentic that we become reconnected to the divine source.

The Tao contains the power to liberate you from the ego-imposed prison of the dualistic world. Living in the Tao can bring a deep inner peace and a reconnection to the divine source. The wisdom of the Tao is in a practical sense, a way to live life with the clarity of knowing the universal truth. When you are living in the Tao, you will see resistance and opposition fade away. Conflict and stress will become distant memories. The issues of life become irrelevant or will simply disappear once you start living your authentic self with the Tao. The Tao shows how to transcend all those insurmountable obstacles that the ego has created.

Doctor Phil does well in explaining the difference between the authentic and fictional {ego} self.

"When you're asked, "Who are you?" what is your answer? "I'm a mom," I'm a doctor." "I live in Texas." Often the answer is not who you are, but what you do, what your social station is, or how you see your function in life. You can't answer who you are, because you don't know.

There is another level of existence that is the real, true, genuine substance of who you are. This is the authentic self. The authentic self is the real you that can be found at your absolute core. It is the part of you not defined by your job, function, nationality, religion, race or role in life. It is the composite of all your skills, talents and wisdom. It is all of the things that are uniquely yours and need expression, rather than what you believe you are supposed to be and do.

When you're not living faithfully to your authentic self, you find yourself feeling incomplete, as if there is a hole in your soul. You may have found that it's easier to fill the roles your family and friends expect of you, rather than becoming who you really want to be. Living this way drains you of the critical life energy you need to pursue the things you truly value.

When you live a life that has you ignoring your true gifts and talents while performing assigned or inherited roles instead, you are living as your fictional self or in other words, your ego."

The ego causes suffering of the authentic self by creating a belief that it is in servitude and in bondage to the body. This servitude and bondage is only an illusion and it cannot destroy the essence of the soul within the authentic self. When the authentic self rediscovers that it is not the body nor tied down to the physical world, it can break free from the shackles of servitude to the ego. In this awakening the illusion of bondage will cease to exist.

Another way to describe the difference between the ego and the authentic self is to imagine that you are an actor. As an actor you are playing a role. This role is cast in a movie that is your life. Your ego is nothing more than the character being played by your authentic self, the actor.

Ah, but there is the conflict. The ego knows that it can get you to forget that you are the actor and make you believe that you are really the character. By making you believe in this lie, this illusion, the ego has gained power over you.

This is why your ego is your worst enemy. The ego doesn't want to lose that power. The ego will do anything to keep you from the truth. It knows that its existence is transitory and it is trying everything it can to attain eternal life which it can't do or have. It is desperate and dangerous; it is fighting for its life.

Within each and every one of us is an inherent deep profound knowing of who we really are. We all have at one time or another questioned our existence because we felt that there was more to life than what we were living. At those times, we knew that there is more to experience and contribute but we were confused and bewildered. This confusion and bewilderment was created by the ego to keep control over us.

When you realize the truth that you are the Actor, that you control the script and can demand a rewrite, then you have regained the power of your authentic self, your true self. With this knowledge you'll be able to keep a healthy balance between the two. Remember that it is just a role you are playing and there will be more roles to play in the future just like you have played in the past.

Be your authentic self. Your authentic self is who you are when you have no fear of judgment. Your fictional {ego} self is who you are when you have a social mask on in order to please everyone else. Give yourself permission to be your authentic self.

When your purpose is aligned with your authentic self and authentic behavior, you'll enjoy serenity, success and significance. You'll become more intuitive and creative. Forgiveness becomes second nature. Peace and harmony rules your days. Within your authentic self, there is a detachment that provides comfort from anything the world can throw at you. In the suspension of judgment comes freedom. In being authentic you will know yourself.

The more you know yourself, the richer and more rewarding your relationships will become. A simple law of man is this, "The degree that you can know someone is in direct relation to how well you know yourself." To know yourself is to know your fellow man. This arises from being your authentic self.

Another quality of living an authentic life is you are more aware of your intuitive nature. Your intuitive state comes from your peripheral consciousness. It is in that state of non-focus, of being in the moment that allows your intuitive nature to come to the forefront. This is a basic principle of the Tao, the un-definable way of life that comes to be when you are in a state of being authentic. It is knowledge without knowing, wisdom by just being. This is only available to the mind that is free from the linear thinking of the ego. Intuitiveness comes from living in the moment, it happens spontaneously, letting the mind make decisions on its own without the need of the ego. This is also known as "non-action."

Verse Thirty Seven of the Tao- *"The way of the Tao is non-action, centered in stillness. Yet nothing is left undone"*

Non-action and being authentic are one in the same; you can't have one without the other. The action of non-action is letting go and going with the flow. Being in this state you effortlessly respond with ease to whatever arises. Being in an authentic state means that you are aware of your true nature. In this state you are connected to the divine source and you are able to maintain your balance and harmony with nature.

An example of action of non-action is breathing or when you eat. You perform these things without the conscious thought of what is involved in doing them. When you eat, there isn't any play by play narrative of, "okay, now take a bite of the steak, just the right size bite; now chew six times, three on each side, now activate the process of swallowing." No, these actions take place automatically without the need of the mind to oversee the event. This is an act of being in the natural world, just like the sea ebbs and flows, just like your breathing. It just happens in accordance with nature. Living an authentic life is living in accordance with nature with nature being an extension of the divine consciousness along with you.

Living an authentic life means understanding these things along with understanding your true nature. By this act alone you'll become more attentive in cultivating your moral character. You'll strive for excellence while living a more virtuous purpose. You'll live a life based in integrity, dignity and peace. In living an authentic life, you'll know peace, love, and joy. You'll live a life full of passion. You'll be living in the Tao.

CHAPTER THREE

THE ART OF LIVING IN ONENESS

Verse Ten of the Tao-*"Embrace your body and soul as one. How can you avoid the separation?"*

Living in the Tao is the art of living in the Oneness. The Oneness cannot be described into any earthly language; it is beyond the words of this world. It isn't about doing, rather it's about being. It isn't about being an identity. In the Oneness, there is no need for an identity. An identity can only exist in separation. In the Oneness, there are no labels as there is no need for them. In Oneness there is no one but the one within the one.

An example of this paradox can be seen in a tree. Sitting here I can see this majestic Oak tree out my window. I see her branches swaying with the breeze while the leaves dance among themselves, giving refuge to the songbirds and squirrels. I know this tree as long as I do not try to bring it into language. As long as it is outside language, I am one with the tree. However, as soon as you ask me about the essence and meaning of the tree, I cannot answer that question because I don't know the tree, at least not in the context of language.

As long as I stay in that state of Oneness, I am one with the tree. When I try to bring the meaning of the tree into the language of a dualistic world, the meaning becomes lost. By putting a label on the tree-- calling it a tree, I have created a separation between the tree and me. In this separation, I lose the connectiveness and therefore the ability to articulate the true meaning. Creating separation is the only way anything can be described. Only by being outside of an object can we put a meaning to it. But as long as we are in Oneness with the object, there is no need for any description.

Can you achieve oneness? The answer is yes. Mindfulness is one of the principles of the Tao. Mindfulness is the art of living in the moment and being in the now. Mindfulness is the mind being in a quiet state, stilled and at peace.

"Like water, which can clearly mirror the sky and the trees only so long as its surface is undisturbed, the mind can only reflect the true image of the Self when it is tranquil and wholly relaxed."- Indra Devi

By practicing mindfulness you can cultivate being in oneness. There are people who have mastered this principle. They can serve as a guide for you. It has been illustrated throughout history in the writings of enlightened men such as Thich Nhat Hanh, Paramahansa Yogananda, Buddha, Rumi, and Christ. Their works are full of examples of living in the moment.

However living in the moment involves a deep and profound paradox. You cannot pursue mindfulness for its benefits. The reason is the expectation of the rewards of being in the moment creates a future-oriented mindset. By applying a future-oriented mindset to the presence, you have negated the state of living in the moment therefore any benefits or rewards that come with it.

Rather, you must trust that the rewards will come. There are many ways to achieve mindfulness and each one contains within itself a paradox. You must let go of what you want in order to get it. To obtain oneness through mindfulness, you must trust in it without striving for it. In order to be, you must stop doing. Just let it happen naturally.

The moment you attain a state of oneness you'll be brought into harmony and balance with the natural world. By realizing the divine consciousness in yourself you'll be able to see it everywhere and in everything. Upon this realization you'll become aware that you are more than just a physical being but rather a spiritual being that is co-creating this universe that we all live in. The empowerment of this realization is profound in the sense that you have become reconnected to the divine source, the Tao. To be in the oneness is to have access to the knowledge and wisdom of the divine. With this new enlightenment you'll see latent possibilities become actualized. Being in a state of oneness is the crown of the Tao.

The essence of the Tao can be seen in verse twenty five,

"There is something supreme and mysterious that has existed before the Heaven and Earth. In the silence and solitude ever unchanging and ever present. Ever extending and ever reaching is the mother of ten thousand things. Her name I know not .This is called the Tao. For the Tao is great. Being great it flows out far away, only to return again. For this is the life breath of all things. The Tao is great, the heaven is great, the earth is great, the people are great. Here lie the four great powers of the universe with man being one of the great things. Man follows the earth, the earth

follows heaven and heaven follows the Tao. And the Tao follows its own nature of being the Tao"

There are two points that the Tao is making in this verse. One, all creation was born out of this divine silence. It is in this silence where the Divine Consciousness resides. The creating power of the divine is omnipresent. It has always been and will always be. Herman Melville was quoted as saying that Silence is God's one and only voice. He also said that all profound things and emotions of things are preceded and attended by Silence. This is illustrated here in verse twenty five. Only what is conveyed in the silence is the truth of the divine. True communication from the divine is always in the form of silence. You might find at first that these communications come in the form of feelings and emotions. This is only another aspect of the divine talking to you through your intuitive self.

The second point to verse twenty five is in order to truly know the way of the Tao you need to know that the greatness of the Tao is already within you. Everything that comes from the Tao is great therefore you are great. We are all an extension of the greatness of the Tao or, God. As it is above, so it is below. Jesus said, "I am in you, you are in me and I am in the father, whatever I can do you can do greater." This the second point of this verse. This verse could very well be the most significant lesson within the Tao. The greatest of God is already within you!

Verse Twenty One of the Tao- *"The greatest virtue is to be one with the Tao- Not by doing but by being, not by striving but by thriving. The Tao is ever elusive and obscure. While vague and elusive it is seeable in its actions. Even though it is dim like the twilight its essence shines. This essence is omnipresent, ever knowing and everlasting, from the beginning before the beginning until now and forever. Creation never ceases, always unfolding, always being. I know this certainty because the Tao is within me..."*

The Tao that cannot be told is in the oneness, a state of unselfish divine consciousness. As long as you are in the Oneness, you are one with all and yet nothing at all. In Oneness there is no up so there is no down. There is no evil so there is no need for good. There is nothing beautiful so there is no need for ugliness. In this Oneness, there is only one. Oneness is a singularity that coexists in the time space continuum of the dualistic world. While a singularity can exist in this time space, a dualistic world cannot exist in the singularity. We are all part of the Oneness living in this illusionary world. We are a living paradox of being a singularity. Jesus said it best when he said, "We are in this world but we are not part of it." To understand this is to know the Tao.

CHAPTER FOUR

THE TAO AND THE ART OF SURFING

Surfing is a wonderful metaphor for describing the Tao. When dealing with the waves of the ocean, you have no control over them nor do you have the ability to enforce your will upon them. The success of a surfer depends on adapting to the situation and going with whatever is presented to him. So it is with life.

Life is like a wave and you're the surfer. So what is a wave? Is it something that you can grasp and hold on to? Is it something that you can take home and put on the fireplace mantle? Can you grab its power and put it in a bottle? The answer to all these is no. A wave is fluid motion. Ever changing and always moving. You can bear witness to it, watch it as it unfolds until it comes ashore but there is no way you can grab it and put it in a bottle. No matter how hard you try to tame it or take hold of it, it cannot be done.

In order to grasp the essence of the wave, you must become one with it, just like the surfer who rides the wave; and just like the surfer; your success totally depends on your understanding of the dynamics and behavior of the wave.

What are the dynamics of the wave? First, you cannot force your will upon the wave nor can you exercise any control over it. You must be malleable to adjust to the wave. You must be a master of balance, be agile, have courage and be able to react instinctively without thought. It is through surrendering to the wave that you are able to become the master of it. It is in the letting go of your own Ego in trying to manipulate and control the wave that you are able to become one with the wave.

In order to become one with the wave you need to learn to live life without the need to possess it. Overcoming the Ego is a requirement in learning to live the Tao. This is the key to living in harmony. Just go with the flow and accept whatever comes your way. A successful surfer practices this principle every time he rides a wave.

Like the Tao, a surfer must find that "middle ground" of the wave to have success. Too early and there isn't enough incline to catch it, too late and you chance getting caught in the concave and ending in a washout. When a wave is caught at the right time, the surfer must always maintain himself in the middle. All the while, he must perform instinctively without hesitation which requires constant commitment.

Tao is achieved when you become an extension of the wave and the wave becomes an extension of you. This is exactly what Lao Tzu was talking about when you overcome by yielding. This is a great example of allowing yourself to be one with the wave by moving naturally, intuitively, automatically, and unconsciously without thought or awareness and without allowing reason or Ego to control the situation.

If we were to fight against the wave, what can we expect? I would say that with the force of the wave it would drag us down and carry us along while we are fighting to regain some sense of control, all the while trying to get and stay on the surface so we can breathe. Imagine the energy that we would need just to get back to some resemblance of control. And in the end, we haven't accomplished anything. To fight against the nature of the wave isn't the way of the Tao.

Living life is like riding the wave. We just need let go and let be. We need to stop fighting the current and learn to go with the flow. It is against our nature to try to control what isn't ours to control. Learn the difference of what you can and cannot control. When you realize the difference you'll change your awareness. In discovering this principle you'll discover your own true nature.

In releasing and relaxing, things will change and become more aligned with nature. You will begin to notice and let go of those things that you cannot control. When you are able to do this, the insurmountable doesn't seem to be so difficult and lows don't appear so low anymore. Life is in a flux of change and ever changing. No matter what you are faced with, you'll know that this too will pass.

CHAPTER FIVE

THE ESSENCE OF NATURE

"As with everything in nature we are already perfect, therefore why seek perfection?"

If you can grasp the essence of Nature, the nature of nature, then you can grasp the essence of the Tao. Nature is perfection at work. Within nature there is a sense of dignity, integrity, and ethics. Nature are these things in itself. It is a supreme example of how dignity, integrity, and ethics are shown through the harmony and balance of nature.

Ethics are the practice of integrity and dignity is the result of this practice. Integrity like the Tao transcends all religions and philosophies. This is the natural way of things; this is the way of the Tao.

In order to get to this state of understanding, you must first deprogram yourself from the belief system you have grown to live by. First of which is to realize that you are already perfect. There is no need to seek what you already possess.

Nature is the manifestation of the divine consciousness. It is the same of all things. From the simplest organism to the most complex forms of life, it is all within itself part of the divine manifestation. Like the countless cells in your body that come together to comprise who you are, so it is with the universe.

But we have been taught otherwise. We are taught that the one with the most toys wins. Whoever scores the most points wins, that winning is paramount. Get ahead at all cost, that's the motto, whatever the cost, even at the expense of walking on the backs of other people, all is fair in love and war and all is fair in the game of life. Yep, that's the ticket, win baby win!

Or worse, we are taught through religion or political dogmas that we are not worthy of the attention of the masters, that we are inferior and doomed to an eternity of damnation because we are separated by this unworthiness from the master.

Only through great sacrifice and servitude or by the grace of these demigods can we hope to receive the crumbs off the master's table. By their grace we might be granted salvation. And why is this so? To keep us separated from our authentic self and to keep their control over us. Napoleon Bonaparte said it well when he said, *"Religion is what keeps the poor from murdering the rich."*

All these beliefs are in direct conflict with nature, with our purpose, and with our authentic self. The purpose of these beliefs is to create separation. These belief systems are the work of the Ego, either yours or someone else's. Power can only come to those by forcing the submission of others to their doctrine and to their ego. The Ego can only exist within this separation. Within the individual the ego forces its will over the soul and the authentic self for control to rule as it sees fit. The Ego knows that in oneness and unity, it cannot survive and will fight to the death to keep you in a state of separation from the oneness.

This is not our nature for us to be so absorbed in this artificial world. It isn't natural to be caught up in a race to the top or to amass control, power or wealth or to manipulate others. To live without regard for our fellow man isn't natural. Selfishness isn't a characteristic of nature nor of the authentic self.

Let us take another look at nature again. In nature, you do not see this behavior. Have you ever seen a squirrel bragging about how many acorns he has amassed? Or a squirrel worried about getting his bonus because he hasn't met his quota for the week? How about a bird claiming to have the biggest bird nest in the tree? I've never seen a rooster showing off how big his hen's breasts are, have you?

I am not saying that motivation or trying to get ahead is a bad thing, but getting so caught up in the race that you forget the reason why you're in the race in the first place, well, that is not living in a natural way.

Being out of balance, living in conflict and in a state of confusion is to live in the artificial world. The road signs of living an unnatural life are depression, anxiety, and stress. Another issue is being unable to trust. It is unnatural to be in a state of not trusting. Without trust, there can be no positive growth.

Isn't it funny that we trust that the sun will rise tomorrow? That without question, we believe in gravity, even though we cannot see it? We know the moon has influence on the tides and we act accordingly. So why can't we trust in the nature of the universe and in ourselves?

There are universal laws that govern all events in nature. All things adhere to these laws without question or concern, existing in peace and harmony while staying balanced. All these things trust in divine consciousness for their purpose and existence.

When we realize that everything is governed by these laws of nature, that these laws not only govern the physical world but the spiritual world we begin to understand our own nature. The physical world is only an extension of the spiritual world. Once we understand this principle, we can have harmony and balance with nature.

But we as a species, will dismiss anything that doesn't conform to what we have been taught. If it doesn't fit into our way of thinking, then it cannot be. This separation is brought about by mistrust. Now the interesting thing about the issue of mistrusting is how can you be sure that you trust yourself to mistrust? That within itself is a paradox. How can you trust yourself to decide what to mistrust? How do you know what truths are real and which ones are not while living in an artificial world?

Verse Twenty Nine of the Tao- *"Those who try to take over the world and rule it in an unnatural way end in failure. The world is sacred and fragile following the way of nature. The way of nature is the way of the Tao. Therefore you cannot improve upon nature. Those who try to change it in the end destroy it"*

In nature all things adhere to the universal laws of nature. In doing so, they live in peace and harmony. We suffer because of our actions, not because of God's wrath or punishment. We suffer because we break the laws of nature. Pure and simple! Suffering is brought about by violating our nature. When we are out of balance with our nature we pay the price by being angry, stressed, confused, and in agony. We are out of balance because we have forgotten to trust in ourselves, to trust in our nature and in nature itself. Being out of balance is to live absent of dignity, without integrity or ethics.

Living in the essence of nature is to trust, to trust in the divine consciousness. Living in the essence of nature provides the best opportunities to learn the principles of the Tao. Living in this essence leads to thoughtful consideration, the mastery of dignity, integrity, and living an ethical life. With meditation, mindfulness, and thoughtfulness, one can learn to live in a natural state with the divine source. To live with nature and understand her is to know the Tao.

CHAPTER SIX

A ROSE BY ANY OTHER NAME IS STILL A ROSE

"The names of things do not matter, only what things are."- William Shakespeare

I want to show the timeless nature of the principles of the Tao. How these principles have transcended time, religion and political dogmas. The underlying message has been the same regardless of who the messenger was. This has been true since the dawn of man. Throughout history there has been a writer, a philosopher, a ruler or an artist that demonstrated the essence and principles of the Tao. It doesn't matter what you call it, a rose by any other name is still a rose. This is the Tao.

Epictetus was a Greek Stoic philosopher who lived from 55AD to 135AD. He was born a slave and became one of the most famous philosophers of his time. Epictetus's Stoic teachings parallel the philosophy of the Tao. Stoicism and the Tao are both very deeply rooted in spiritually.

Epictetus believed in obtaining a higher awareness of the innerconnectiveness of mankind to all living things and to the universe. Epictetus is one of the key figures of Stoic philosophy and emphasized that virtue is sufficient for happiness.

The basis of his philosophy is that all external events are determined by fate and are out of our control. But we do have the power to accept whatever happens to us in a calmly manner. However individuals are responsible for their own actions which they can and should control. By self-discipline one can become master of controlling their fate. He also taught how it is our responsibility to care for all human beings. He is very consistent in his teachings about man's connection to one another and to nature. He believed followers of this philosophy would achieve happiness and that the joy of life is in the journey.

Another Stoic philosopher, Marcus Aurelius, who is considered to be the most spiritual ruler of all the emperors of Rome, wrote a book called, "Meditations." It is a book based on the philosophy of service and duty. It describes how to find and preserve equanimity in the midst of conflict by following nature as a source of guidance and inspiration. It's not just a set of beliefs; it is a way of life involving practice and discipline. Constant contemplation and the process of living these beliefs is the life of a Stoic. Stoicism is a spiritual practice of staying in the present, of staying attentive to your actions and of self-reflection using logic and reason as a foundation.

What is interesting about contemplation is that in Mysticism, contemplation plays an important part in attaining higher states of consciousness. Through contemplation, one is able to stay on the path. This is a key principle of the Tao, contemplation.

Several of the basic tenets of Stoic philosophy are very similar to the principles of the Tao. Let's take a look at a few of these Stoic tenets. "Live life with ethics, virtue, and honor." "Freedom is secured not by the fulfilling of men's desires, but by the removal of desire." Another one, "Outward things cannot touch the soul, not in the least degree; nor have any admission to the soul, nor can they turn or move the soul; but the soul turns and move's itself alone." And lastly, "Virtue is nothing else than right reason, pursue it to the hilt."

The Tao can be found in Jewish Mysticism. In the Zohar, one of the texts of Jewish Mysticism one can find references to the Tao. Jewish Mysticism deals with the "Law" which is very similar to the Tao. Their belief is if one can be one with the Law, then his eternal salvation is assured by being in that oneness. The paradox of this belief is by being in a state of oneness; you are already in a state of eternity.

Within the Zohar, concerning spiritual progression in the here and hereafter, the Zohar states that the soul of a man who has consecrated himself to the study of the Law will upon leaving his earthly body go to a blissful abode by the pathways of the Law, so that his knowledge acquired on earth is of use to him in the hereafter, but those who have willfully neglected to obtain knowledge go astray along roads that lead to "Geburah," a state of suffering. Symbolically speaking the Law acting as the guardian and protector goes before the soul which has delighted itself in sacred study and opens all celestial doors before it. The Law clears the path for the soul to follow and the Law remains with the soul until the day of resurrection when it will serve as the soul's defender.

The Mystic Jews call it the law, the Christians call it God, the Pagans call it several different names but in the end, they are all describing the same thing, a divine consciousness. Once you learn the essence of the Tao, you'll begin to see it in everything and everywhere.

Ralph Waldo Emerson is an excellent example of someone that lived in harmony with nature and with the Tao. Throughout his life he demonstrated time and time again living within the Tao. He was often referred to as the "Concord Sage" during his lifetime and for good reason. These Taoist tendencies are very noticeable in his writings. An example of this can be found in his essay, "The Oversoul," first published in 1841. Here is an excerpt from his essay,

"We live in succession, in division, in parts, in particles. Meantime within man is the soul of the whole; the wise silence; the universal beauty, to which every part and particle is equally related, the eternal ONE. And this deep power in which we exist and whose beatitude is all accessible to us, is not only self-sufficing and perfect in every hour, but the act of seeing and the thing seen, the seer and the spectacle, the subject and the object, are one. We see the world piece by piece, as the sun, the moon, the animal, the tree; but the whole, of which these are shining parts, is the soul."

Here we see his thoughts on the oneness of the universe, the innerconnectiveness of nature, the power of silence and living as a whole in a dualistic world of which are all contained in the Tao.

As a leading philosopher of the transcendentalist movement during the 1800's Emerson brought forth ideas on creative intuition, self-reliance, and the individual's own unlimited potential. He was instrumental in bringing awareness and enlightenment to his fellow men. He believed that by transcending the limits of rationalism and the perceived tradition of his time, one could fully realize their potential.

His views which were the basis of transcendentalism suggested that God does not have to reveal the truth because the truth could be experienced intuitively directly from nature. His beliefs were all things are connected to God and, therefore, all things are divine. As you can imagine his religious views were often considered radical among the religious leaders of his time. However his views and beliefs are very reminiscent of the way of the Tao.

One of the most compelling pieces that Emerson wrote concerning the importance of the connection with nature was from one of his early lectures that became the foundation for his first published work known as the essay, "Nature." Here is an excerpt from that 1836 essay,

"Nature is a language and every new fact one learns is a new word; but it is not a language taken to pieces and dead in the dictionary, but the language put together into a most significant and universal sense. I wish to learn this language, not that I may know a new grammar, but that I may read the great book that is written in that tongue."

Emerson knew the way of the Tao and the power contained within nature. Whether he knew of the Tao or not, I don't know but it is evident by his work and his life that he was definitely living the principles of the Tao.

An interesting facet of Emerson's personal relationship with nature was shared by his son, Doctor Edward Emerson, some years later after his father's death. The Doctor was asked about his father's method of writing. His reply is quite insightful and remarkable into the power of his father's connection with nature. He said,

"It was my father's custom to go daily to the woods to listen. He would remain there an hour or more in order to get whatever there might be there for him that day. He would then come home and write into a little book, his "day-book," of what he had gotten. Later on, when it came time to write a book, he would transcribe from this, in their proper sequence and with their proper connections, these entrances of the preceding weeks or months. The completed book became virtually a ledger formed or posted from his day-books."

It seems that Emerson had found the very heart and soul of God, of the Tao within nature while being in those woods. I would venture to say that Emerson had found a way to listen to the divine in the silence. In those moments, he was one with nature, connected with the Tao. It was the knowledge and wisdom of the Tao that allowed him to communicate with the divine. This is an excellent example of living in the essence of nature.

Another example would be the works of John Burroughs, an American naturalist who was important in the evolution of the conservation movement in America. Burroughs was heavily influenced by the works of Ralph Waldo Emerson and equally influenced by his love of nature. His biographer, Edward Renehan said that Burroughs was a literary naturalist with the duty to record his own unique perceptions of the nature world. To illustrate his views of nature I submit this passage from, "The Summit of the Years" which was published in 1913.

"I am in love with this world; by my constitution I have nestled lovingly in it. It has been home to me. It has been my point of outlook into the universe. I have not bruised myself against it, nor tried to use it ignobly. I have tilled its soil. I have gathered its harvests, I have waited upon its seasons and always have I reaped what I have sown. While I gathered its bread and meat for my body, I did not neglect to gather its bread and meat for my soul."

Another excerpt that shows his sense of wonderment and reverence for nature is from the essay, "The Heart of the Southern Catskills," published in the late 1880's.

"The works of man dwindle, and the original features of the huge globe come out. Every single object or point is dwarfed; the valley of the Hudson is only a wrinkle in the earth's surface. You discover with a feeling of surprise that the great thing is the earth itself, which stretches away on every hand so far beyond your ken."

In reading the writings of John Burroughs you see a profound spirituality in his views of nature. For Burroughs to have such a deep and profound respect and love for nature, he must have had that connection of oneness that the Tao speaks of. While John Burroughs might have not known of the Tao, his writings say otherwise.

Herman Melville is best known for his novel, "Moby Dick" which is considered to be one of the most important American literary masterpieces of the twentieth century. He was very spiritual and had a keen insight into the connection between the nature of man and the nature of nature. It is evident in his writings such as his belief that the one and only voice of God is silence. Here is one of his comments about nature and the innerconnectiveness of man,

"We cannot live only for ourselves. A thousand fibers connect us with our fellow men; and among those fibers, as sympathetic threads, our actions run as causes, and they come back to us as effects."

This is a very fair representation of the principle of the innerconnectiveness of nature as in the Tao. Melville's understanding of nature and man are based in the Tao and again, I doubt he knew of the Tao.

Another snapshot into the soul of Melville can be seen in this excerpt from a letter he wrote to Nathaniel Hawthorne in the summer of 1851,

"We shall sit down in Paradise in some little shady corner by ourselves; and if we shall by any means be able to smuggle a basket of champagne and if we shall cross our celestial legs in the celestial grass that is forever tropical, and strike our glasses and our heads together till both ring musically in concert: then, O my dear fellow mortal, how shall we pleasantly discourse of all the things manifold which now so much distress us."

While this illustrates Melville's mood of serene desolation at the time, it's a skeptically humorous outlook at man's vanity of gloating over frivolous victories that are worthless outside this domain. It is as if he is laughing at the absurdity of man. He is quoted as saying as much, *"Whatever my fate, I'll go to it laughing."*

At the time he wrote this letter he was only 32 years old and had already lived more life than most men could only dream of. He also had achieved literary success and fame. But in it all he seemed to realize that life was nothing more than an exercise of experiencing being a human. He knew there was more to life and had discovered in his adventures the key to what that more was. He had a distinct connection and love for nature along with an understanding of the illusion of this world. This can be seen in this quote from Moby Dick,

"Me thinks we have hugely mistaken this matter of Life and Death. Me thinks that what they call my shadow here on earth is my true substance. Me thinks that in looking at things spiritual, we are too much like oysters observing the sun through the water, and thinking that thick water the thinnest of air. Me thinks my body is but the lees of my better being. In fact take my body who will, take it I say, it is not me."

Melville's views on obtaining happiness and meaning should not be in the pursuit of some mythical in the sky religious account of the order of things but rather through our actions and relationships with one another and with nature. He believed the meanings one derives from being dedicated to "The wife, the heart, the bed, the table, the saddle, the fire-side, the community, the country," are the genuine meanings of life. The acquiring of these meanings are enough to overcome any threat on the eternal life and by these meanings one's life will not dissolve into a series of meaningless events. When an individual commits to living a life of meaning it is deserving of admiration even if it doesn't fit the tradition of Christianity.

Melville's approach seems to recognize that the presence of the many distinct and good ways of life was something that could and should be strived for. He felt that it would be highly beneficial for a person to search and attain these meanings. In other words, live a virtuous life with respect for one another. While these beliefs are similar to Stoic philosophy and the Tao, I believe it is relevant to point out that the Tao can be disguised in many forms. In using Melville's own words to prove the point,

"Truth is in things, and not in words."

George Carlin! Yes, I said George Carlin. I didn't throw this in just to see if you are paying attention. Nope, George Carlin is part of this group too. Part of understanding the Tao is realizing the reality of the illusion that we are living in. "Getting it" is a big part of the Tao and George Carlin got it. He offered his perspective of how he viewed the world in the form of comedy.

In a way he was our generations' version of Mark Twain. I believe in less than fifty years from now his comedy routines will be taught in philosophy classes in universities throughout America. His Taoist nature was to show us the absurdity of our actions but he failed in believing that we would see the truth hidden in his humor. Given time, some of us have figured it out and now realize what a treasure we had in him.

Carlin had a side to him that has been forgotten that offers an insight into his connection with the Tao. I want you to think about these comments. I want you to see his soul. It is important for you to learn not to dismiss someone because they don't fit the guidelines of what is acceptable. Sometimes it is these people that are on the outside of society that have the best view. Here are a few of his views through his axioms:

1-Throw out non-essential numbers. This includes age, weight and height. Let the doctors worry about them. That is why you pay them.

2- Keep only cheerful friends. The grouches pull you down.

3- Keep learning! Learn more about the computer, crafts, gardening, whatever, even ham radio.

4- Never let the brain idle. "An idle mind is the devil's workshop." And the devil's family name is Alzheimer's.

5- Enjoy the simple things. Laugh often, long, and loud. Laugh until you gasp for breath.

6- The tears happen. Endure, grieve, and move on. The only person who is with us our entire life is ourselves. Be ALIVE while you are alive.

7- Surround yourself with what you love, whether it's family, pets, keepsakes, music, plants, hobbies, whatever. Your home is your refuge.

8- Cherish your health. If it is good, preserve it. If it is unstable, improve it. If it is beyond what you can improve, get help.

9- Don't take guilt trips. Take a trip to the mall, even to the next county; to a foreign country but NOT to where the guilt is.

10- Tell the people you love that you love them at every opportunity.

11- Capitalism tries for a delicate balance: It attempts to work things out so that everyone gets just enough stuff to keep them from getting violent and trying to take other people's stuff.

12- I'm having fun because I don't take life seriously – the only things I care about are my family, friends, work and my lady, Sally. Philosophers for a long time have said 'Why are we here?' – I'm here for the entertainment. If you're born in the world, you're given a ticket to the freak show; if you're born in America, you get a front row seat.

And one more from George,

"Life is not measured by the number of breaths we take, but by the moments that take our breath away. And if you don't send this to at least 8 people — who cares? But do share this with someone. We all need to live life to its fullest each day!"

There is so much we can learn from all these people about life if we would only take the time to look and listen. To borrow from George; we all need to learn to live life to its fullest every day!

CHAPTER SEVEN

JOHN LENNON, IMAGINE AND THE TAO

"When I was 5 years old, my mother always told me that happiness was the key to life. When I went to school, they asked me what I wanted to be when I grew up. I wrote down "happy." They told me I didn't understand the assignment and I told them they didn't understand life." - John Lennon

Was John Lennon aware of the Tao? Yes he was! On the cover of "Give Peace a Chance," a book based on John and Yoko's bed-in for peace interviews, there is a photo of them reading "The Way of Life according to Lao Tzu." John and Yoko learned as they went along, searching through the wisdom of Lao Tzu for guidance during this time in their lives.

I want to believe that the Tao had a profound effect on John and in part continued to drive his desire for world peace. I am sure Lennon had his own demons to deal with but he did display an uncanny sense of the Tao. His works showed a deep introspective view of life and a sense of awareness beyond his years. I believe that he viewed his life as a work of art and lived his life accordingly.

Of all the songs he wrote there is none more relevant or better suited to serve as the anthem for the Tao then "Imagine." Imagine conveyed Lennon's wish for world peace and harmony in simple terms, both musically and lyrically. It is a basic message, asking for freedom from hunger, religion, and suffering.

Imagine is considered an international anthem of peace. Just about everyone has heard this song. It transcends religion, race, age, culture or anything else that separates people. Former President Jimmy Carter had this to say about the song,

" In many countries around the world - my wife and I have visited about 125 countries - you hear John Lennon's song 'Imagine' used almost equally with national anthems."

The Tao deals with the art of living in the moment; this is seen clearly in this verse,

"Imagine there's no heaven. It's easy if you try .No hell below us, Above us only sky. Imagine all the people living for today."

The Tao transcend all religions and dogmas. The Tao deals in living in peace and harmony with each other, as seen in this verse,

"Imagine there's no countries. It isn't hard to do. Nothing to kill or die for. And no religion too. Imagine all the people living life in peace."

The Tao teaches trusting in yourself and following your own path independent of what others think. This is seen in this verse,

"You, you may say I'm a dreamer, but I'm not the only one. I hope someday you'll join us. And the world will be as one."

The Tao stresses the importance of being free from the trappings of the materialist world and not to fall victim to greed and selfishness. This is evident in this verse,

"Imagine no possessions. I wonder if you can. No need for greed or hunger. A brotherhood of man. Imagine all the people sharing all the world"

John Lennon captured the essence of the Tao with this song. He said he was influenced by a book that Yoko Ono wrote called Grapefruit. The inspiration for the song began with a poem from that book called Cloud Piece,

"Imagine the clouds dripping. Dig a hole in your garden to put them in."

Here are his words on the origins of the song. Within the quote you'll see John admitting to having issues with his ego at one time and the sense of remorse for his actions. It is interesting to see his spiritual growth through the interviews he gave over the years. Lennon was well on his way of becoming a Taoist Master.

"The song was originally inspired by Yoko's book Grapefruit. In it are a lot of pieces saying, Imagine this, imagine that. Yoko actually helped a lot with the lyrics, but I wasn't man enough to let her have credit for it. I was still selfish enough and unaware enough to sort of take her contribution without acknowledging it. I was still full of wanting my own space after being in a room with the guys all the time, having to share everything."

There is no doubt that towards the end of Lennon's life he began to show a more spiritual side and his longing for world peace. It is no secret that he along with George Harrison were searching for the deeper meaning of life. While he had to work out his own problems with life, I believe that he was following his purpose and the path that was meant for him. While he could be abrasive and crass at times, the message was always there.

Following is an excerpt of an interview that came out in the January 1981 Playboy magazine. This is to give you more insight into John Lennon's way of thinking. David Sheff had a candid conversation with John and Yoko Ono. You'll see with this brief interview that Lennon was indeed on the path of the Tao.

David Sheff: *What is the Eighties' dream to you, John?*

Lennon: *Well, you make your own dream. That's the Beatles' story, isn't it? That's Yoko's story. That's what I'm saying now. Produce your own dream. If you want to save Peru, go save Peru. It's quite possible to do anything, but not to put it on the leaders and the parking meters. Don't expect Jimmy Carter or Ronald Reagan or John Lennon or Yoko Ono or Bob Dylan or Jesus Christ to come and do it for you. You have to do it yourself. That's what the great masters and mistresses have been saying ever since time began. They can point the way, leave signposts and little instructions in various books that are now called holy and worshiped for the cover of the book and not for what it says, but the instructions are all there for all to see, have always been and always will be. There's nothing new under the sun. All the roads lead to Rome. And people cannot provide it for you. I can't wake you up. You can wake you up. I can't cure you. You can cure you.*

David Sheff: *What is it that keeps people from accepting that message?*

Lennon: *It's fear of the unknown. The unknown is what it is. And to be frightened of it is what sends everybody scurrying around chasing dreams, illusions, wars, peace, love, hate, all that -- it's all illusion. Unknown is what it is. Accept that it's unknown and its plain sailing. Everything is unknown -- then you're ahead of the game. That's what it is. Right?*

As you can see Lennon's views were complex to say the least. He harbored anger at the establishment for the manipulation of mankind, just read the lyrics of "Working Class Hero" to see his views. But he held out hope that change could come around without violence as he was a proponent for peace.

Another aspect of Lennon was his thoughts on what is and isn't considered real. He seemed to have developed a sense of this world being an illusion, a thin veil hiding the truth. I believed that he had come to the conclusion that we were nothing more than sheep that was being controlled by a hand full of people. I believed that before his death, he discovered oneness with the divine consciousness and was on a path to show others the way.

This quote from him explains this rather well.

"I believe in everything until it's disproved. So I believe in fairies, the myths, dragons. It all exists, even if it's in your mind. Who's to say that dreams and nightmares aren't as real as the here and now?"

And lastly, Lennon believed in this one thing, the one thing that is required in order to move towards a more meaningful peaceful way of life free from the warring and conflicts that surrounds us today, and that one thing we all need, in his words is, " All you need is Love."

CHAPTER EIGHT

NATIVE AMERICANS AND THE UNIVERSAL NATURE OF THE TAO

There have been groups of people throughout history who have lived in the way of the Tao. The Native Americans are a great example of a group who strived to live in the way of the Tao. This shows the universal nature of the Tao of how when people live in accordance with the laws of nature, they naturally move towards living a more authentic life.

One only needs to look at the beliefs of the Native Americans to see the evidence of their profound respect of nature. The Native Americans would only kill animals for food or in defense, never for sport. They would never cut down a living tree for firewood unless there were no other options. They had respect for all living things because they knew the innerconnectiveness of the universal consciousness.

They considered themselves caretakers of their domain. They never saw themselves as owners with the right to do whatever they felt like doing. They maintained their respect for nature, which was first and foremost in their lives. They considered themselves responsible for how they leave the land for at least the next 7 generations. In the western world, I doubt most people think about they are doing next year much less what kind of legacy we are leaving for our grandchildren's grandchildren.

The Native Americans have an understanding of the innerconnectiveness of life and nature. It is engrained into their belief system. For a group of people with no organized structure or resemblance to the Western world, they seem to have a deep profound knowledge of the mysteries of life.

They lived in peace and harmony not only with their fellow man but with nature. Black Elk is quoted for saying this about peace,

"The first peace, which is the most important, is that which comes within the souls of people when they realize their relationship, their oneness with the universe and all its powers, and when they realize that at the center of the universe dwells the Great Spirit, and that this center is really everywhere, it is within each of us."

People who are in the Tao are called Sage's. It is important to know what a Sage sounds like when he speaks. One of the most famous Native American Sages was Chief Seattle. There is a speech that is reported to have been given by Chief Seattle in 1854. It was in response to a proposed treaty which the Indians were persuaded to sell two million acres of land for $150,000.

I first heard the speech in 1988 when it was recited by Joseph Campbell. Campbell was an American writer best known for his work in comparative mythology and religion, author of several books including "The Power of Myth." His philosophy is often summarized by his famous quote, "Follow your bliss."

At the time I heard this speech I was moved by the eloquence, insight and depth of the words. It was beautiful and profound in the way these thoughts were expressed with such vividness. It wasn't until I discovered the Tao that I realized how similar these two philosophies were. It was at this time I realized that the Tao is most definitely universal. This was a moment of clarity into the meaning and nature of the Tao.

Following is the text of Chief Seattle's famous speech. This provides an excellent example of how a Sage communicates with his fellow man. See if these words have an effect on your soul.

"How can you buy or sell the sky, the warmth of the land? The idea is strange to us.

If we do not own the freshness of the air and the sparkle of the water, how can you buy them?

Every part of this earth is sacred to my people. Every shining pine needle, every sandy shore, every mist in the dark woods, every clearing and humming insect is holy in the memory and experience of my people. The sap which courses through the trees carries the memories of the red man.

The white man's dead forget the country of their birth when they go to walk among the stars. Our dead never forget this beautiful earth, for it is the mother of the red man. We are part of the earth and it is part of us. The perfumed flowers are our sisters; the deer, the horse, the great eagle, these are our brothers. The rocky crests, the juices in the meadows, the body heat of the pony, and man --- all belong to the same family.

So, when the Great Chief in Washington sends word that he wishes to buy our land, he asks much of us. The Great Chief sends word he will reserve us a place so that we can live comfortably to ourselves. He will be our father and we will be his children.

So, we will consider your offer to buy our land. But it will not be easy. For this land is sacred to us. This shining water that moves in the streams and rivers is not just water but the blood of our ancestors. If we sell you the land, you must remember that it is sacred, and you must teach your children that it is sacred and that each ghostly reflection in the clear water of the lakes tells of events and memories in the life of my people. The water's murmur is the voice of my father's father.

The rivers are our brothers, they quench our thirst. The rivers carry our canoes, and feed our children. If we sell you our land, you must remember, and teach your children, that the rivers are our brothers and yours, and you must henceforth give the rivers the kindness you would give any brother.

We know that the white man does not understand our ways. One portion of land is the same to him as the next, for he is a stranger who comes in the night and takes from the land whatever he needs. The earth is not his brother, but his enemy, and when he has conquered it, he moves on. He leaves his father's grave behind, and he does not care. He kidnaps the earth from his children, and he does not care. His father's grave, and his children's birthright are forgotten. He treats his mother, the earth, and his brother, the sky, as things to be bought, plundered, sold like sheep or bright beads. His appetite will devour the earth and leave behind only a desert.

I do not know. Our ways are different than your ways. The sight of your cities pains the eyes of the red man. There is no quiet place in the white man's cities. No place to hear the unfurling of leaves in spring or the rustle of the insect's wings. The clatter only seems to insult the ears.

And what is there to life if a man cannot hear the lonely cry of the whippoorwill or the arguments of the frogs around the pond at night? I am a red man and do not understand. The Indian prefers the soft sound of the wind darting over the face of a pond and the smell of the wind itself, cleaned by a midday rain, or scented with pinon pine.

The air is precious to the red man for all things share the same breath, the beast, the tree, the man; they all share the same breath. The white man does not seem to notice the air he breathes. Like a man dying for many days he is numb to the stench. But if we sell you our land, you must remember that the air is precious to us, that the air shares its spirit with all the life it supports.

The wind that gave our grandfather his first breath also receives his last sigh. And if we sell you our land, you must keep it apart and sacred as a place where even the white man can go to taste the wind that is sweetened by the meadow's flowers.

So we will consider your offer to buy our land. If we decide to accept, I will make one condition - the white man must treat the beasts of this land as his brothers.

I am a savage and do not understand any other way. I have seen a thousand rotting buffaloes on the prairie, left by the white man who shot them from a passing train. I am a savage and do not understand how the smoking iron horse can be made more important than the buffalo that we kill only to stay alive.

What is man without the beasts? If all the beasts were gone, man would die from a great loneliness of the spirit. For whatever happens to the beasts, soon happens to man. All things are connected.

You must teach your children that the ground beneath their feet is the ashes of our grandfathers. So that they will respect the land, tell your children that the earth is rich with the lives of our kin. Teach your children that we have taught our children that the earth is our mother. Whatever befalls the earth befalls the sons of earth. If men spit upon the ground, they spit upon themselves.

This we know; the earth does not belong to man; man belongs to the earth. This we know. All things are connected like the blood which unites one family. All things are connected.

Even the white man, whose God walks and talks with him as friend to friend, cannot be exempt from the common destiny. We may be brothers after all. We shall see. One thing we know which the white man may one day discover; our God is the same God.

You may think now that you own Him as you wish to own our land; but you cannot. He is the God of man, and His compassion is equal for the red man and the white. The earth is precious to Him, and to harm the earth is to heap contempt on its creator. The whites too shall pass; perhaps sooner than all other tribes. Contaminate your bed and you will one night suffocate in your own waste.

But in your perishing you will shine brightly fired by the strength of the God who brought you to this land and for some special purpose gave you dominion over this land and over the red man.

That destiny is a mystery to us, for we do not understand when the buffalo are all slaughtered, the wild horses are tamed, the secret corners of the forest heavy with the scent of many men and the view of the ripe hills blotted by talking wires.

This is the end of living and the beginning of survival."

Last of these examples of the native people living the principles of the Tao is by Chief White Cloud. I want to share a little wisdom from this great Sage.

"Your religious calling was on plates of stone by the flaming finger of an angry God.

Our religion was established by the traditions of our ancestors, the dreams of our elders that are given to them in the silent hours of the night by the Great Spirit, and by the premonitions of the learned Beings.

It is written in the hearts of our people, thus: We do not require churches which would only lead to us to argue about GOD. We do not wish this. Earthy things may be argued about by men, but we never argue over GOD.
And the thought that white men should rule over nature and change its ways following his liking was never understood by the Red man.

Our belief is that the Great Spirit has created all things. Not just mankind, but all animals, all plants, all rocks... For us all, life is holy. But you do not understand our prayers when we address the sun, moon, and winds. You have judged us without understanding, only because our prayers are different. But we are able to live in harmony with all of nature.

All of nature is within us and we are part of all nature."

CHAPTER NINE

A SINGULARITY IN A DUALISTIC WORLD AND LANGUAGE

A singularity existing in a dualistic world is a paradox within itself. The foundation of language and the nature of linguistic meaning is the very basis of philosophy in the dualistic world. With the Tao, language doesn't apply, hence the paradox. I hope to show how this paradox can be overcome by showing the differences of the two and how it applies to the Tao.

So how does a singularity exist in a Dualist world? Here is an illustration: Take a magnet, it has a South Pole and North Pole. No matter how many times you cut that magnet in half, it will always have a South and North Pole. You cannot escape the essence of duality, no matter how small the magnet becomes, there is always a South Pole and North Pole.

However, in the center of that magnet lies a place where there is no South or North Pole. You cannot see it, you cannot detect it but it is there. It is there that singularity exists, in that place between the two conflicting forces. It is in this center of the dualistic world, between the up and down, the left and right, or good and evil where an unknown and unseen center exists. It is that center where there is singularity and this is where the Tao resides.

Living in the Tao is to know the Divine Consciousness. Being in the Tao is to co-existence in this world and the realm of the Divine Consciousness. It is in the singularity where the Divine Consciousness resides.

There is a relationship between language and the dualistic world. Language by its very nature supports and reaffirms the constructs of duality by making a signifier, [symbol] represent a signified, [a concept or meaning as distinguished from the symbol it represents]. Confusing? It gets better. If a signifier exists without pointing to or representing a signified then it is regarded as meaningless.

Our minds tend to think that there is a class of things which are symbols and a class of things which are not but there is not a clear distinction between a signifier and the signified. A signified may itself be a signifier pointing to another signified and the physical object to which the idea refers is merely another symbol. Is your head spinning yet? What very few realize is that if I showed you a picture of a kitty cat you would still only see a symbol of a constructed class of animals, not the individualism of the cat.

So what does all of this mean? First, the Tao resides in the "singularity" of the Divine Consciousness while we live in the "dualistic world." In this world we suffer from self-imposed separation from the singularity. Our separation is brought on by our ego and our ego uses language as its operating system to maintain the separation. In order to break free from the constraints of the dualistic world we must break free from the destructive nature of language and its representation. Only then can we access the "singularity" of the Tao.

This is the science behind of the meaning of the first verse of the Tao, "The Tao can be told is not the eternal Tao." In a very deep sense, only what is repressed is symbolized, because only what is repressed needs to be symbolized. The magnitude of symbolization shows how much has been repressed and buried. Anything that we are not in a conscious relationship with will possess us.

Having a conscious relationship with the Tao requires no use of language. It is beyond words. Being in the oneness of the Tao is to know what non-verbal communication is.

Chuang Tzu illustrated this principle with this saying,

"The fish trap exists because of the fish. Once you've gotten the fish you can forget about the trap. The rabbit snare exists because of the rabbit. Once you've gotten the rabbit, you can forget about the snare. Words exist because of meaning. Once you've gotten the meaning, you can forget the words. Where can I find a man who has forgotten the words and meaning so I can talk with him?"

Unfortunately most people never get past this precept in order to experience the oneness of the divine consciousness within the singularity of the universe. This is in part due to the way we use and see language.

Language and the Tao- The issue with language is in order to understand it, you must first have a relationship to whatever object is being experienced or discussed. That relationship comes from your own experiences, and based on those experiences, it depends on how you interpret the meaning of the object with words. Then there is still only an external description of the object.

Let's look at the word tree. To a carpenter, it is a source of lumber; to a tired traveler, it provides shade; and to a landscape architect, it is a decorative piece to be used in a landscape design. To a newspaper, it is a source of paper for printing more newspapers. Another one, the word, "Bark," until you have the context in which the word is used, you don't know if we are talking about tree bark or the bark of a dog. The point is, it depends on your perspective as to what anything means to you.

Even then, language can still fall short of describing an event or a task. Describing something can never take the place of the actual experience. Even a task as simple as tying one's shoe laces is an endeavor using language. Try to explain or write down how to tie a shoe lace to a child who has never done this before. Since this child has never had a relationship with this task, you'll always fall short of getting the information across in an effective manner. No matter how hard you try to explain this task into words, you just cannot get it done as effectively as by demonstration.

The best approach is to simply show the child how to tie their shoelaces. Through the action of example, one is able to convey the meaning of the task. By showing someone how to do it, you're able to drive the point home. This is where the Tao seems paradoxical because one cannot be taught all the different perspectives of a dualistic world. In order to truly know, you must experience it for yourself. The real meaning cannot be conveyed by being separated from the experience. To understand the Tao, there cannot be any separation; the Tao doesn't exist outside of oneness. Only in Oneness, can one see all and be all.

This is how the Tao is taught, by action and example. Someone who has no knowledge of the Tao will still recognize a Sage living in the Tao. They may not be able to put their finger on it but there is an awareness they will have, maybe even intuitive, to inform them that something special is taking place. Only by seeing can one begin to start on the path of the Tao. Now this is the funny thing: the Tao is everywhere; it is in plain sight. The Tao is not hiding from anyone; it is right here, right now. All that is required to see it is to have an awareness of its existence.

CHAPTER TEN

THE DISCONNECTION FROM NATURE

Verse One- *"Those who live in the state of desire see only the external illusion of manifestation"*

The issue with today's society is that we have forgotten our connection to nature. Now it's all about how much can you can accumulate and how far can you get ahead. We have lost touch with the natural aspects of being human and have turned life into a game of getting all you can while you can without regard for anyone else. We have become so absorbed in this rat race we have become disconnected from our authentic self.

Our values have become compromised. Our gods today are called Sony, Samsung, and LG. We can't wait to get home to pay homage to these gods to see what wonderful news is waiting for us. Our desires and goals are to see the events of American Idol, The Bachelor, or Dancing with the Stars. We have become as a society; in the words of Oscar Wilde,

"Most people are other people. Their thoughts are someone else's opinions, their lives a mimicry, their passions a quotation."

We have lost our sense of value in ourselves, in each other and in our society. We have become like sheep, following whatever is placed in front of us. We have become disconnected from nature to the point where most of society doesn't even exist anymore. They are nothing more than shadows cast about with no direction or purpose. In the opening lines of the song "Vultures" John Mayer points out this reality all too clearly with his observation, *"Some of us, we're hardly here. The rest of us, we're born to disappear."*

Verse Seventy Two- *"When men no longer have a sense of awe, disaster will follow as men will begin to look outward from themselves for guidance as they no longer trust themselves. In this guidance they will be led astray by a clever ruler"*

Even today's religions are failing in saving mankind. They are a walking contradiction of their own belief system. The core belief of these religions is the belief of a non-materialist heavenly world. The contradiction in their actions is in order to compete for followers they offer material pleasures and worldly treasures while selling the belief in this non-materialist world. They entice the seekers in search of salvation and redemption with the promise of a mythical paradise that is always beyond their reach.

These followers and seekers are like sheep. They have surrendered their power in exchange for a ticket to a ship that will never sail. The Elitist within these religions have created the separation needed to disconnect the followers from their authentic beings. The sad aspect for these followers is they gave away their power unknowingly to the very people that they now need for guidance in searching for the place that they already possess.

Gandhi talked about living in a corrupt system and what should be done to correct it. Here is a quote from him on this subject,

"You assist an evil system most effectively by obeying its orders and decrees. An evil system never deserves such allegiance. Allegiance to it means partaking of the evil. A good person will resist an evil system with his or her whole soul"

If this is the case then how are these systems of corruption thriving today? How could the masses be so disconnected?

There is a very good reason for this disconnect from nature. Why is there such a great divide between the human species and nature? Simple! Take a look at the human species. We are the only species on this planet that acts and behaves in the manner that we do. My theory on this unusual anomaly is that as a species we have been domesticated. Because we have been domesticated we are living in an artificial world, a world that is not meant for us. Living in an artificial world is the root cause of all our problems.

If left alone, people would gravitate back to living in a natural way without conflict, greed or strife. Here is an interesting example of what man can do if left to his own accord. This story is by Irving Wallace, David Wallichinsky and Amy Wallace. It is from an article that was published in Parade Magazine about an event that happened during World War One.

"Among the horrors of World War One, there occurred a unique truce when, for a few hours, enemies behaved like brothers. Christmas Eve in 1914 all was quiet on France's Western Front, from the English Channel to the Swiss Alps. The trenches came within 50 miles of Paris. While the war was only 5 months old, there had been approximately 800,000 men wounded or killed. But something happened; British soldiers raised "Merry

Christmas" signs and soon carols were heard from German and British trenches alike.

Christmas dawned with unarmed soldiers leaving their trenches, as officers of both sides tried unsuccessfully to stop their troops from meeting the enemy in the middle of no-man's land for songs and conversation. Exchanging small gifts—mostly sweets and cigars—they passed Christmas Day peacefully along miles of the front. At one spot, the British played soccer with the Germans, who won 3-2.

In some places, the spontaneous truce continued the next day, neither side willing to fire the first shot. Finally the war resumed when fresh troops arrived, and the high command of both armies ordered that further "informal understandings" with the enemy would be punishable as treason."

This story is noteworthy because it reveals that man isn't naturally prone to war. If left on their own, they would gravitate towards living in peace. If not for the high command threatening treason punishable by death, I would guess these soldiers would have lay down their guns and walked away. I would like to imagine they wanted to, wanted to go back to a peaceful life with their families, living their lives in pursuit of more meaningful things.

It was the pressure of an artificially created structure by the "powers to be" that caused these soldiers to return to fighting. The fighting was by design by the rulers, not by the will of the common man. In spite of the "powers to be," even for a brief few hours, the Tao was alive and well along those trenches. For a few moments, these men were living in their authentic life, the life that they wanted and longed for. This is the reason for the Tao, to show us the way back to the world that we belong.

The bigger question is why we were domesticated to begin with. Look at it this way: what is easier to manage, a thousand head of cattle or ten wild mustang ponies? We are all living under the same pressures of an artificial social structure, all arising out of unknown factors. There's been a long-fought psychological war against your mind, but why?

One only needs to look at the education system to see an example of why this is being perpetrated. In 1918, Alexander Inglis wrote in his book, Principles of Secondary Education, that the education system was designed to "produce a population deliberately dumb down and declawed in order that government might proceed unchallenged and corporations might never want for obedient labor."

In 1924 H.L. Mencken wrote an article for "The American Mercury"- "The aim of compulsory schooling is to reduce as many individuals as possible to the same safe level, to breed and train a standardized citizenry, to put out dissent and originality. That is its aim in the United States...and that is its aim everywhere else."

More recently in 2009, Colonel John B Alexander, Director of the Advance Systems Concepts Office of the US Army Laboratory Command had this to say when asked why so many people do not believe in the existence of the paranormal or in the research of paranormal projects by the US Army, "We have through the western education system taught that it can't be so therefore it isn't." He goes on to suggest that this system is by design.

There is a reason for the way things are in our society. Whatever the reason, the Tao serves as a roadmap to get us back to the world that we came from, to reconnect to the divine source. It is that world where the laws of nature are upheld and kept, a world where man is allowed to live in peace and harmony.

This controversial theory is a subject that could take up an entire book. I only mention it as an example of why the Tao is so needed today. Study the nature of man for any length of time and I am sure you will come to the same conclusions.

CHAPTER ELEVEN

WHAT DOES AWAKENING TO THE TAO LOOK LIKE?

The legendary environmentalist Aldo Leopold had an extraordinary career. He was instrumental in shaping and influencing the modern environmental movement. His ethics of nature and wildlife preservation has had a deep and profound impact on the environmental movement with his bio-centric and holistic ethics regarding land and nature. Of equal importance he founded the science of wildlife management. He stressed the importance of biodiversity and ecology in order to preserve and ensure a harmonic balance between wildlife and the land. Even though it has been over sixty years since his death, Leopold remains relevant today inspiring projects and people by bringing about an awareness and connection to the land.

However, Aldo Leopold wasn't always the stalwart crusader for the environment. His awakening and enlightenment to the Tao came to him in a moment of clarity. In an instant, his eyes became opened and his soul reborn. Following is an excerpt from his book, "A Sand County Almanac," which was published shortly after his death in 1949. It has sold over two million copies which is phenomenal in its own right. In this passage, you'll see the transformation of an egotistical outdoorsman into an enlighten guardian of nature.

Thinking like a mountain- *"A deep and chesty bawl echoes from rimrock to rimrock, rolls down the mountain, and fades into the far blackness of the night. It is an outburst of wild defiant sorrow, and of the contempt for all the adversities of the world.*

Every living thing and perhaps many a dead one as well pays heed to that call. To the deer it is a reminder of the way of all flesh, to a pine a forecast of midnight scuffles and of blood upon the snow, to a coyote a promise of gleanings to come, to the cowman a threat of red ink at the bank, to the hunter a challenge of fang against bullet. Yet behind these obvious and immediate hopes and fears there lies a deeper meaning, known only to the mountain itself. Only the mountain has lived long enough to listen objectively to the howl of the wolf.

Those unable to decipher the hidden meaning know nevertheless that it is there, for it is felt in all wolf country, distinguishes that country from all other land. It tingles in the spine of all who hear wolves by night. Or who scan their tracks by day. Even without sight or sound of wolf, it is implicit in a hundred small events: the midnight whinny of a pack horse, the rattle of rolling rocks, the bound of a fleeing deer, the way shadows lie under the spruces. Only the ineducable tyro can fail to sense the presence or absence of wolves, or the fact that mountains have a secret opinion about them.

My own conviction on this score dates from the day I saw a wolf die. We were eating lunch on a high rimrock, at the foot of which a turbulent river elbowed its way. We saw what we thought was a doe fording the torrent, her breast awash in white water. When she climbed the bank toward us and shook out her tail, we realized our error: it was a wolf. A half dozen others, evidently grown pups, sprang from the willows and all joined in a welcoming melee of wagging tails and playful maulings. It was literally a pile of wolves writhed and tumbled in the center of an open flat at the foot of our rimrock.

In those days we never heard of passing up a chance to kill a wolf. In a second we were pumping lead into the pack, but with more excitement than accuracy; how to aim a steep downhill shot is always confusing. When our rifles were empty, the old wolf was down, and a pup was dragging a leg into impassable slide-rocks.

We reached the old wolf in time to watch a fierce green fire dying in her eyes. I realized then, and have known ever since, that there was something new to me in those eyes- something known only to her and to the mountain. I was young then, and full of trigger-itch; I thought that because fewer wolves meant more deer, that no wolves meant hunters' paradise. But after seeing the green fire die, I sensed that neither the wolf nor the mountain agreed with such a view."

The impact of his own gunshot from a rimrock that day in Arizona changed Aldo Leopold's thinking in an instant. In a moment one man's way of thinking was changed with such profound awakening that it has permeated throughout all conservation efforts. The impact of this seemingly routine event brought about a deep contemplation into the insight of his relationship with all living things. This life changing event has touched the lives of so many since then.

I doubt very seriously if Leopold had not had this sudden perception of the essence of nature or in other words, an epiphany, we would not be discussing him now. This is the point, the only point I am making here. No matter how you perceive yourself to be, no matter how you may think of yourself being significant or insignificant, no matter how clever you may think you are, you're wrong!

With an awakening, a burst of enlightenment or an epiphany, you can radically change not only your life but the lives of others for years to come. Awakening means letting go of old beliefs that cannot exist in a state of divine unconditional love. This is the power of the Tao.

These moments are all around us, just waiting for us to realize and act upon them. But you cannot see what you are not looking for. Begin today to start looking for your epiphany. Begin your path with the Tao and start living a life more authentic and more in harmony and balance with the Divine. Drop the attachment to the ego and learn to use it to your benefit. Become more aligned with your true purpose and start living the life that was meant for you. Live it to the fullest with passion, joy and love for this is the way of the Tao.

CHAPTER TWELVE

THE TAO FROM A CHRISTIAN PERSPECTIVE

From a Christian perspective one can see the Tao. But it is only visible when the religious dogma and manipulation has been removed and eliminated so the true essence can shine through. The point here is to show that the Tao can be seen in Christianity. By realizing that the universal nature of the Tao is everywhere, even in whatever religion you may practice, by seeing the divine consciousness in everything, in knowing that nature and the soul are one and the same, you can deepen your own sense of connection with the Divine Consciousness.

Several of the tenants and principles of the Tao are clearly seen here in this passage from Henri Frederic Amiel's Journal. He touches on the connection of nature and the soul, of being in the "oneness" of the Tao, or for Christians, the "oneness" of God. To understand this passage is to know how to see the many faces of the Tao. To know the Tao is to know God. To know the Tao is to be a Taoist and be free.

"Every landscape is a state of the soul, and he who reads in both marvels at the likeness in every detail. True poetry is truer than science, because it is synthetic and grasps at once what the combination of all sciences can only attain at best someday in the future. The poet divines the soul of nature; the scientist only serves to accumulate the materials for demonstration. The one rests in the whole, the other lives in a particular region. The one is concrete, the other abstract.

The soul of the world is more open and intelligible than the individual soul; it has more space, time and strength to manifest itself.

The most beautiful of poems is life: life which is read and composed at a single breath, in which fancy and conscience are allies and aid each other, life that knows it is a microcosm and rehearses in miniature, in the presence of God, the universal, divine poem.

Yes, be man, that is, be nature, be Spirit, be God's image, be what is greatest, most beautiful, most elevated among all the spheres of being, be an idea and an infinite will, a reproduction of the great whole. And be all by being nothing, by effacing yourself, by letting God enter into you as air enters a vacant space, reducing your selfish ego until it is only a vessel that contains the divine essence. Be humbled, composed, silent, that you may hear in the depths of yourself the voice that is subtle and profound; be spiritual and pure, that you may enter into communion with the pure spirit.

Withdraw often into the last sanctuary of your innermost consciousness, re-enter your atomic punctuality, that you may be freed from time, space, matter, temptation, dispersion, that you may escape from your organs and your own life; die often, in other words, and question yourself in the presence of this death, as a preparation for the last death.

He who can confront, without a shutter, blindness, deafness, paralysis, disease, betrayal, want, he who, without trembling, can face the sovereign Justice, he only can say that he is prepared for death, whether partial or total. How far from this am I, how far my heart is from this stoicism! But at least to detach oneself from everything that can be taken from one, to accept everything as a loan and a gift, to cling only to the imperishable, this is something that must be attempted. To believe in a good and fatherly God, a God who educates us and tempers the wind to the shorn lamb, who punishes only when it is necessary and takes away our joys with regret; this thought, or rather this conviction, gives courage and security.

Oh how we need love, tenderness, affection, kindness, and how vulnerable we are, we immortal, sovereign sons of God! Strong as the world, or weak as wisdom only. It is when one is disinterested that one is strongest, and the world lies at the feet of him whom it cannot tempt. Why? Because the spirit is lord of matter, and the world belongs to God. "Be of good cheer," a heavenly voice said; "I have overcome the world."

Thanks, leisure, thanks, retirement; thanks, Providence! I have been able to return to myself, able to give audience to my good angel. I have renewed myself in the feeling of my vocation and my duty, in the remembrance of my frailty. Come new year, bring what you will, but do not take my peace from me; leave me a clear conscious and hope in God!

CHAPTER THIRTEEN

LIVING YOUR PURPOSE

"The mystery of life is not a problem to be solved, but a reality to be experienced"- Soren Kierkegaard

The benefit of living in the Tao is to know your authentic purpose. Therein lies the problem. Humans are the only species that wander throughout life without a clue as to their authentic purpose. More than likely, your purpose, the one that is meant for you, isn't the one that was pressed upon you by your family or by tradition. Your authentic purpose is that calling-that passion that lives within you. Maybe you have experienced it; a burning desire that you should be doing something more with your life other than whatever it is you're currently doing.

Abraham Maslow said that it is necessary to live life independent of the good opinions of others. This is another primary precept of the Tao: to live your own Tao, to live your purpose. Discovering and living your purpose is one of the first steps on the path of the Tao. Once you realize to trust yourself and follow your path--your calling, and your passion from within, then and only then will you be able to start to live in the Tao.

In nature there is no judgment. There is no living by the opinions of others, there is only living. All living creatures in nature live life without the concern or fear of what others think of them. They have no attachment to the outcome of their actions. They are living in the moment, removed from any thought or judgment to their actions. It is a continuing exercise of actions without reactions. In other words, they are just doing and being what it is that they are. This behavior is called *living your purpose*.

Another word for living your purpose is "Dharma." When you are living your purpose, there is no need for ambition or motivation. The passion of living your Dharma is more than enough to compel and propel you to act. When you are living your purpose you are on the path of the Tao.

What does your life look like when you are living your purpose? When you're living your purpose, you're like a puzzle piece that fits perfectly. Everything seems to be the way it should be, and when it isn't, it doesn't matter because you know that even in seemly bad times it is still part of your purpose and part of your journey. No matter where you are in life, you know that this too will pass. It is all transitory; you just go with the flow.

When you are living your Dharma, you are following your own intuitive nature. You find yourself leaving reason and intellect behind in favor of following the truth from within. Intuition is defined as an instinctive and unconscious knowing without the need for deduction or reasoning. It operates outside the boundaries of conventional reasoning and away from the constrictive nature of the Ego. Living your purpose is your best defense against the artificial world. The power of intuitive understanding will protect you from the harms of the world. This is living in the Tao.

Another aspect of living your purpose is to understand this precept, "Be kind to the kind and kind to the unkind." When you master this principle it will become second nature to you. You'll just go with the flow knowing that this is part of your nature of being in the moment. All that comes your way is by design and serves a purpose. This is living in a state of acceptance within your purpose. In Zen Buddhism, this is called living in the ordinary mind. An ordinary mind or "natural mind" is one that is in the present, whatever the state of emotions or consciousness, whatever the nature, living without the realization of being in the moment. What a beautiful concept to live in.

One way to cultivate being kind to the unkind is to learn to see yourself in everyone you meet. Take a day and make it a point to focus on everyone you meet. Look at them and try to see yourself in them. Imagine life through their eyes. Try to find a connection to everyone you see. Study their mannerisms; do you see yourself in them? Realize that we are just like pieces of a puzzle. Everyone is playing a role in life and has a reason and purpose for being here. Look for that reason for being and realize that all these roles are necessary for the picture to be complete. Just like the 50 trillion different cells in your body, each one playing a part in making you whole, so it is with the universe.

No matter how much society may succumb to groupthink and thought control or the adverse effects of being "Politically Correct," always look for the human spirit. It will always try to come through one way or another. Man cannot force the soul to stay buried in the dark depths forever. The infinite consciousness within all of us will at some point come through and prevail over the illusionary veil that has been thrown over society. This is the

Tao, knowing the difference between the two and choosing to live life in the natural world, the world of divine consciousness.

The choice we need to make is whether to trust in our own nature, to be of a pure heart and mind or to live in a world where we are trying to control everything. We have seen that going against our nature provides no comfort or satisfaction for our souls. For authentic satisfaction, for true peace, we must learn to realize who we are and where we came from. The truth is all around us. You can hear the voice of god in the laughter of children at play and in the songs of the birds. You can see God in all his glory throughout all of nature. It is all around us to see and experience. Remember you are part of this universe and here to experience it. Be your Authentic Self and be one with it all. To live in the Tao and live your purpose is to live life to the fullest.

To close, I want to leave you with this question, "What if God manifested himself through us, through his creation, in order to experience himself?" And in order to truly experience it fully, he had to forget who he was. Could this be the Tao, a remembrance of who we really are? May your journey be blessed!

Lao Tzu's Tao Te Ching

An Interpretation

Verse One

The Tao that can be spoken is not the true Tao.

The names that are given do not contain their true meaning

Within the nameless is the true meaning

What is named has a mother and she is the mother of ten thousand things

The un-seeable is always seeable within the internal to those who are not bound by desire

Those who live in a state of desire see only the external illusion of manifestation

These two opposites are born from the same source

The source contains its mystery in darkness

Within the darkness is the darkness that is the gateway to the mysteries

Verse Two

All that is on the Earth residing under the Heavens that is beautiful is only beautiful because of the ugliness that coexists with the beautiful

There can be only good if there is evil

Difficult is the opposite of easy therefore they complement each other. The long and the short are related. The high and the low are related. Song and words are related. The front and the back are related

This relationship is the balance of the world as they come and go

The Sage is able to do without doing, teach without speaking

The ten thousand things come and go without interruption

Life and death, creating without possessing, staying in balance with nature

Accomplishing without taking credit, moving forward forgotten. Therefore lives forever

Verse Three

Desiring not to possess or accumulate which is only temporal

Desiring not to covet the treasures of the world

These actions prevents temptation- stealing, jealously, ambition and quarreling

These actions keep the heart and mind pure.

The Sage with a pure heart and mind is at one with the Tao

Therefore free from the trappings of the world he is able to show the way

By emptying their hearts of desire and keeping their bellies full. The people are simple and free therefore the cunning and the clever cannot interfere

All may live in peace and balance where there is action without interference

Verse Four

The Tao is like a vase that is empty yet used

It is the emptiness that gives birth to the vase

This emptiness, deep and unfathomable, is the source of the ten thousand things

It dulls the sharp

Unties the knots

Softens the light

Subdues the chaos

While hidden always present

Not knowing the source or from where it came, it has always been here since before time, for it is timeless

Verse Five

Heaven and Earth act without intention or benevolence and are not moved or swayed by offerings of straw dogs

The Sage acts in accordance to the same laws of nature and is not moved by offerings of straw dogs

For nature follows the Tao and so the Sage, all is equal under the sun, all is treated without regard or condition, offering his gifts to all

Heaven and Earth are like bellows, empty yet inexhaustible

As the work of the bellows is increased, so is the production increased

Through these actions the Sage remains tranquil and centered, sitting quietly while seeing the truth within

So with you. Stay centered with your thoughts

Verse Six

The valley spirit never dies

For she is the mystic divine mother containing the perfection of the universe. In all the forms of the mystic divine mother, her essence is never changing

For she is the gateway to all creation from which Heaven and Earth were born, her power always remaining unbroken

In the silence you will hear her without fail

In the stillness she will reveal her mysteries

Draw upon her wisdom as drawing water from a well, gently as her well is everlasting

Verse Seven

The Heaven is everlasting and the Earth last forever

Why is this so?

For the Heaven and Earth does not exist for its own sake

This is their secret

Like the Heaven and Earth, the Sage too lives the same, putting himself last

By doing so, the Sage becomes first, through being unselfish and serving the needs of others

Fulfillment is assured.

Verse Eight

The highest good is like water

Water brings life to ten thousand things, bringing nourishment without striving. It seeks out the lowest levels to settle, places that people avoid and despise

This is like the Tao; water is in accordance with nature

The Sage is like water, living his life in accordance with nature, going with the flow of life. The Sage seeks humble refuge, in meditation staying true without desire. He is thoughtful in his relations with his fellow man, keeping an open heart

The Sage is gentle in his nature, standing by his word and actions, sincerity and honestly precedes him in his travels and dealings. Always governing with equality, being timely and competent in his endeavors

Staying in balance and harmony with nature, the Sage lives the way of the Tao

Verse Nine

Better to stop pouring before the brim of the cup, for it is easier to hold an unfilled cup than a cup that is overflowing

Sharpen a sword to its sharpest edge and the edge will soon grow dull

Fill your house with gold and jade and you'll find it hard to protect

To desire fame, wealth, and honor is to bring about a downfall of your own doing

When your work is done, then retire

The Sage seeks neither fame nor fortune

Withdrawing once the work is done in a natural manner

This is the way of the Tao

Verse Ten

Embrace your body and soul as one

How can you avoid the separation?

Can you allow your nature to be like that of a new born baby and be in harmony? Can you begin to see with clarity the mystic vision? Can you love your fellow man without judgment? Can you rule the land without need of fame?

Playing the feminine part, can you open and close the gates of Heaven?

Can you see all throughout the land and people without interfering? Can you control your Ego and stay within your authentic self?

Give birth and nourish without attachment, To have without the need to possess. To create and give without need of the credit, Leading without being dominating. Leading by example rather than rule

This is the mystical way of the Tao

Verse Eleven

Thirty spokes connect at the center of the wheel at the hub

It is the center of emptiness of the hub that makes the wheel useful

When shaping clay, it is the emptiness that creates the vase

It is in the emptiness that makes it useful

Rooms are made to have doors and windows

The usefulness of the room depends on what is not there

Without a door, a room cannot be entered

Without a window, there is no light

The usefulness of what exist depends on what doesn't exist

Such is the essence of non-existence

Verse Twelve

The five colors blind the eyes

The five sounds deafen the ears

The five flavors deaden the taste

Excessive desires will madden the mind

Excessive possessions preoccupy the mind with fear

The more you desire, the more you'll be discontented from what you have.

The Sage fills his belly, not his eyes

The Sage satisfies his inner desires with what cannot be seen, not with the external temptations of the world

Verse Thirteen

Meet failure or success with grace, honor and kindness

Accept misfortune or fortune with grace, honor and kindness.

Why?

Do not be concerned with either. Accept all that comes your way. Good and evil comes from having a body, which is the cost of being human. Good or evil cannot affect the true essence of the soul

The soul of man is everlasting. Surrender yourself and love all that comes your way. See yourself in all that comes your way

See the divine perfection in the Mother of the universe. Know that you are one with all

In doing so you will be trusted to care for all things

Verse Fourteen

What cannot be seen is invisible

What cannot be heard is inaudible

That which cannot be held is intangible

These three are beyond definition. Therefore they are as one

With no form or sound, they cannot be described

As they are from the nothingness that is unseen, unheard and untouchable

There is no light at rising. There is no darkness at setting

It continues in a place where there is no time or space

Embrace it and you'll find no beginning or end

You cannot know it but you can be part of it

Embrace the experience beyond words and feel the essence of the Tao

Verse Fifteen

The ancient masters of the Tao were subtle and mysterious

Their knowledge and wisdom was beyond that of the common man

It is difficult to describe these men, only by their appearance

Watchful and aware with no fear

Acting as a guest upon the earth in their travels

They were unpretentious, dignified, sincere, courteous, yielding, receptive, and pure of heart

Clarity comes to muddy waters by being stilled

In being tranquil in the stillness brings about peace from the chaos

The Sage of the Tao doesn't seek fulfillment therefore he is not affected by desires

Verse Sixteen

Empty yourself completely

Bring your mind to rest and your heart to peace

Allow the ten thousand things to come and go while just observing

See how one ending is just another beginning

See the serenity in the movement to and fro from the divine source

Come to know the eternal wisdom by returning to the divine source and realize your destiny

For this is the enlightenment of the Tao

Knowing that all is everlasting

Even after the death of the body, you will remain whole in the Tao

Verse Seventeen

The existence of the most exalted and revered leaders are barely known among men

Next comes the leaders who are loved and praised

Next comes those leaders who are feared and despised

A leader is trusted as much as he trust his fellow man

The exalted speaks little or carelessly

The exalted are wise in their words and actions

The exalted know the value of seeing their task completed by making it appear to have happened in a natural way

So the people will proclaim that the events happened by their own accord

The exalted have no need for praise or credit, no need to possess

Verse Eighteen

When the great way of the Tao is forgotten

Benevolence and Righteousness will become prevalent

Then wisdom and logic will be born

Bringing about great pretense and hypocrisy followed by disorder

When harmony and balance cease to exist and man has lost his way

The virtue of caring for one another and love will arise from the chaos

At these times loyal servants will appear

Verse Nineteen

If we could renounce and do away with wisdom, knowledge, religion and cleverness then it would be a hundred times better for everyone

Do away with morals and justice and people will begin to do the right things. Give up the desire for wealth and thieves and robbers will disappear

These three forms of governing are insufficient

More important is living in a simple manner within one's own nature and keeping the well-being of others at heart

Living an unpretentious life with compassion and keeping your desires tempered is to live in your own true nature

This is the way of the Tao

Verse Twenty

Abandon learning to put an end to your troubles. What is the difference between yes and no? What is the difference between good and evil? Are the fears of man truly merited? Or is it all nonsense?

In the spring some go to the park and enjoy a feast, While I wander about alone not knowing where I am, Like a newborn child who has yet to smile their first smile

I am alone belonging nowhere, unattached and homeless. Others have too much, more than they need, striving for fame and fortune, While I have nothing, embracing the shadows and relishing the solitude

Others are full of intellect and knowing with their cleverness and cunning, While I am dumb and dull and play the fool with no worries or concerns. I drift about like a wave on the ocean or like a cloud in the sky while everyone is consumed with their daily life

But I am different

For I am nourished by the great mother

Verse Twenty One

The greatest virtue is to be one with the Tao

Not by doing but being, not by striving but by thriving

The Tao is ever elusive and obscure

While vague and elusive it is seeable in its actions

Even though it is dim like the twilight, the essence shines

This essence is omnipresent, ever knowing and everlasting

From the beginning before the beginning until now and forever

Creation never ceases, always unfolding, always being

I know this certainty because the Tao is within me

Verse Twenty Two

Yield like water and overcome

Bend like a Palm tree to remain straight. Be empty like a vase to be full. Death brings rebirth

To have little leaves room for more. Those who have too much are troubled. The Sage embraces humility to serve as an example for his fellow man

The Sage is free from the desire of needing recognition. Therefore his example shines brightly. His distinction comes not by force or assertion

He is powerful not by ruling with a heavy hand. He is chief in not having pride. He doesn't compete therefore no one can compete with him. The ancient Sages say "Yield to overcome"

Stay whole and all things will come to you

Verse Twenty Three

To speak little is natural

High winds do not last the morning. Thunderstorms do not last all day Why is this so? It is the Heaven and Earth

If the Heavens above and the Earth below cannot make these things eternal

Then how can man? The one that follows the Tao is always one with the Tao

The one that is virtuous knows virtue by experience. Those who don't follow the way of the Tao are lost and feel abandoned

Those who follow the way of the Tao are embraced by the Tao. Those who are at one with virtue will always have virtue with them. Those who are lost are embraced by abandonment

Those who cannot trust themselves will not be trusted by others

Verse Twenty Four

If you stand on your toes, you cannot stand in a steady fashion

If you run at an unnatural speed, you will not be able keep up the pace

One who brags of being enlightened is not

One that is self-righteous is not respected by others

Striving to bring attention to oneself for the sake of gain doesn't last and he will fall in despair

To the followers of the Tao these traits of bragging, self-righteous, and striving are unnecessary and are considered excesses

Followers of the Tao have no need of these traits and will avoid them

Verse Twenty Five

There is something supreme and mysterious that has existed before the Heaven and Earth

In the silence and solitude ever unchanging and ever present.

Ever extending and ever reaching is the mother of ten thousand things

Her name I know not. This is called the Tao. For the Tao is great. Being great it flows out far away, only to return again. For this is the life breath of all things

The Tao is great, the heaven is great, the earth is great, the people are great

Here lie the four great powers of the universe with man being one of the great things. Man follows the earth, the earth follows heaven and heaven follows the Tao

And the Tao follows its own nature of being the Tao

Verse Twenty Six

Gravity is the foundation for light

Stillness is the master of movement

The Sage that travels the day does not lose sight of his belongings

Along the way there are beautiful things to see but the Sage remains detached and stays indifferent choosing to keep his inner peace

Why should a king of ten thousand chariots not take his acts seriously?

For not to take ones duty with sincerity is to lose one's foundation

Not to practice stillness is to lose one's control

Verse Twenty Seven

A Sage is a skilled traveler leaving no trace of his tracks

A Sage is a skilled speaker leaving nothing to be corrected in his words. A Sage is like a skilled accountant needing no audit. A Sage is like a door made pure needing no lock for it cannot be opened. For what a Sage can bind cannot be unbounded

Therefore the Sage is always skillful in helping his fellow man, abandoning no one. He is the caretaker of all things, abandoning nothing

This is the way of the Tao. A good man is a teacher to the bad man. A bad man is a student for the good man

If there is no honor for the teacher or for the student then confusion will arise no matter how clever the confusion is disguised. Therefore this is the essence of the mystery

Verse Twenty Eight

Know the strength of a man while keeping the essence of a woman

Keep your mind like a stream and let virtue flow unimpeded. Be like a child free from the illusions of the world

Know the white by knowing the black. Be an example of virtue to the world. Be an example to the world to see and follow

Staying true without wavering and stay ever unchanging. Staying on the path returning to the infinite. Practice honor but keep your humility, living in the Tao

Become the valley of the world where virtue flows, ever true and ever flowing returning to the simple way of nature like an uncarved block

When an uncarved block is carved, it becomes useful. When the Sage uses it he becomes a ruler. Therefore a great tailor cuts little

Verse Twenty Nine

Those who try to take over the world and rule it in an unnatural way end in failure

The world is sacred and fragile following the way of nature

The way of nature is the way of the Tao. Therefore you cannot improve upon nature

Those who try to change it in the end destroy it. Those who try to grasp it cannot hold it

The way of nature is such that things sometimes are in front and sometimes behind

Sometimes strong and sometimes weak, sometimes hot and sometimes cold

Therefore the Sage avoids the extremes and does away with extravagance and indulgence

Verse Thirty

Those who instruct rulers of the world in the way of the Tao does so by being opposed to conquest by battle or arms

For battle begets battle, force begets force. Thorns and briars follow in the footsteps of marching armies

Violence brings only more violence. Battle, conquest, and force is not the way of nature

The Wise field commander who achieves his adjective does not continue. He only strikes as a necessity, not for the glory or to boast. He strikes only as a last resort, not for pride

Always guarding himself against being arrogant or displaying vanity. For he knows these things are not the ways of nature. Those who go against the way of nature will perish

The way of nature is the way of the Tao. For what goes against the Tao is assured an early death

Verse Thirty One

Weapons of war represent fear among men and are hated by all creatures

Followers of the Tao detest the use of them. The wise leader considers the left to be honorable

While mongers of war prefer the right. Weapons of war are not for the wise

The wise only uses these weapons when it cannot be avoided. The wise practice restraint and caution in the use of them. Never does the wise see glory in their use

Those who relish and celebrate in the killing have lost their way of the Tao. The act of war is like a funeral and should be mourned as such with sorrow and grief

Even for the victorious there should never be rejoicing for there is no good in this type of death

Verse Thirty Two

The ever unchanging Tao has no name. Though it is small, simple, and subtle it cannot be grasped

If the kings and leaders could grasp the meaning of the Tao then the ten thousand things would obey their commands, Heaven and Earth would become united and a gentle rain would fall without judgment towards anyone

Man would become free from the need of laws as all men would live in harmony with nature

Once the one becomes divided there is a need for naming all the parts. There are already too many names

Knowing when to stop frees one from failure and trouble.

The Tao of the world is like a river flowing back to the great sea of divine source

Verse Thirty Three

Wisdom is in knowing others

Enlightenment is in knowing yourself

Force is required to overcome others

Strength is required to overcome yourself

Those who are content with their wealth are rich in the knowing of the Tao

Those who live their purpose live long

Those who live in the Tao live forever

Verse Thirty Four

The great Tao is everywhere, both to the left and to the right

The Tao gives all to the ten thousand things denying none

In fulfilling its purpose the Tao makes no claim or makes any assumption of being the lord of the ten thousand things, instead the Tao remains silent in its works

The ten thousand things always return to the Tao knowing that the Tao isn't their lord

By not showing greatness is truly great

The Sage is like the Tao, by not making himself great his greatness is attained

Verse Thirty Five

The Sage that is one with the Tao is at peace and will have the world come to him

Those who are in the presence of the Sage will experience the peace, calmness and happiness of the Tao

Music and merriment are only passing pleasures yet people partake of such festive activities but how empty and hollowed compared to the Tao

When you look for it, you cannot see it, when you try to hear it, it cannot be heard but when you use it, it is beyond being exhausted

Verse Thirty Six

That which is to be contracted first must be expanded

That which would be weakened must first be strong

That which would fall down must first be raised above

That which would be taken must first be given

This is the nature of things

The weak overtakes the strong, the soft overcomes the strong

Like fish that should not leave the water

Neither should the weapons of a country be displayed

Verse Thirty Seven

The way of the Tao is non-action, always centered in stillness

Yet nothing is left undone

If the rulers of the world knew the way then the ten thousand things would follow their path according to the way of nature

For when things are simple, they return to the simplicity of formless nature

Without form there is no desire

Without desire there is peace in the stillness

Within this stillness is the natural way of the world

Verse Thirty Eight

A man of virtue who is not aware of his virtue is truly a man of virtue. A foolish man who tries to be of virtue is not a man of virtue

A man who is truly wise and of virtue seems to do nothing but leaves nothing undone. The foolish man who is always trying to do, leaves much undone. The man of virtue acts without regard to himself or with condition

The highest form of kindness is that which is given without regard to himself or without condition. The highest form of morality is that which has no judgment or motive

When the Tao is lost then there is virtue. When Virtue is lost then there is morality. When Morality is lost then there is ritual

Ritual is only an empty shell of humanity like a flower and not the fruit; this is the beginning of the downfall of man

The great Sage follows his own nature and not that of society, following the fruit not the flower, he stays with the truth while rejecting the false

Verse Thirty Nine

These things from the ancient times come from the one. The sky is whole and clear because of being of the one. The earth is whole and firm because of being of the one. The spirit is whole and complete because of being of the one

The ten thousand things are whole because of the one. Kings and rulers are whole and the land is kept whole. All these things are virtuous from being in the one. The one being the Tao

If the sky wasn't so it would fall. If the earth wasn't so it would cave in. If the spirit wasn't so it would falter. The rebirth of the ten thousand things prevent their death, Kings and rulers keep the virtue of the lands by it

Therefore being humble is the foundation of greatness. The low is the foundation of the high. Kings and rulers call themselves "orphaned," "worthless," and "alone"

Is this an admission on their part of being humble? The individual parts of a carriage does not define a carriage for a carriage is more than the total of its parts. The Sage does not wish to be seen as jade rather to be seen as common stone

Verse Forty

Returning is the way of the Tao

Yielding is the way of the Tao

The ten thousand things are born of being

Being is born of non-being

Verse Forty One

When the wise student hears of the Tao, he practices it with sincere earnest. When the student in the middle hears of the Tao, he may or may not follow the teaching

When a foolish student hears of the Tao, he mocks it, making fun of it with ridicule. If the fool doesn't mock and ridicule it then it would not be the Tao

The path of enlightenment seems dark. Going forward appears to be moving backwards

The easy way seems to be hard. Virtue appears to be hollow. Strength seems weak. The great square has lost its corners

Great powers often come late. Great music is hard to hear. The greatest of all has no form. The Tao is obscure and is without name. The Tao is the nourishment that fulfills everything

Verse Forty Two

The Tao produce the one

The one brought two and the two brought three. It is the three that brought the ten thousand things

The ten thousand things are in the shadow and in the light

By the breath of these two harmony is brought into being

Man doesn't like to be "orphaned," "worthless," and "alone" Yet this is how kings and rulers describe themselves

For in gaining, one loses. For in losing, one gains

What others teach, I also teach, A violent man will die a violent death. This is the essence of my teachings

Verse Forty Three

The weakest of things in the universe can overcome the strongest of things in the universe

That which has no substance can enter where there is no room

I know this is the value of non-action

Few are those who understand teaching without words or work without doing

Verse Forty Four

What is most important? Is it fame or life?

What is more treasured? Is it wealth or life?

What is more painful? Is it gaining or losing?

The man attached to fame and wealth will suffer

By gaining the man will still lose

The man contented is free from shame and danger and never disappointed

A contented man who practices restraint will be safe in all of his years

Verse Forty Five

The greatest perfection seems imperfect yet its purpose cannot be exhausted

The greatest fullness seems empty yet it is ever endless

The greatest straightness seems crooked

The greatest intelligence seem stupid

The greatest eloquence seems awkward

Action overcomes the cold

Stillness overcomes the heat

Stillness, purity, and humility makes everything right in the order of the universe

Verse Forty Six

When the Tao is practiced in the world, horses haul manure

When the Tao is discarded from the world, horses are used in war

The greatest sin for man is desire

The greatest misfortune for man is discontentment

The greatest violation for man is coveting that of others

Therefore the man being in a state of contentment is always contented

Verse Forty Seven

Without going outside the Sage knows everything that is outside

Without looking out the window he knows the Tao under the heavens

The farther one goes from himself the less he knows

Therefore the Sage has his knowledge without the need of traveling

Giving the right names to those things he doesn't see

He accomplishes his purpose without doing

Verse Forty Eight

He who is devoted to learning strives to increase his knowledge everyday

He who is devoted to the Tao seeks to decrease his doing everyday

He does less and less until there is nothing left to do

Once he has achieved non-action, there is nothing which he does not do

All things on earth are ruled by letting them follow their own nature

Things cannot be ruled, nothing can be gained by interfering

Verse Forty Nine

The Sage is not mindful of himself. Rather he is mindful of the needs of others

To those who show goodness to me, I reply with goodness

To those who show evilness to me, I reply with goodness

For virtue is goodness. Those who are faithful, I have faith in them

Those who are not faithful, I have faith in them

For virtue is faithfulness. The Sage is humble and appears indifferent and impartial

People everywhere look upon and listen to the Sage

For the Sage hears and sees like a little child

Verse Fifty

Men come upon the earth to live and die

Three in ten will follow life. Three in ten will follow death. Three in ten will just pass through from birth to death, some barely here and others are born to disappear

What is the reason for this? Because they live in their ego, not knowing their authentic self

The man who is aware of the Tao and walks in the Tao knows his authentic self and lives life with the laws of nature without fear or concern

In battle, he cannot be brought down by weapons. In conflict, he cannot be harmed by adverse actions. Not by a tiger or a rhinoceros can harm come to him

How is this possible? For death cannot enter him as he is above and beyond death. His life is eternal for he lives in the Tao

Verse Fifty One

All things are created by the Tao and are nourished by virtue

Things take their shape according to their nature

The ten thousand things honor the Tao and are grateful for virtue

Not because it is required by the Tao but freely given because this is the nature of things

Therefore it is the Tao that creation comes from. By virtue all things are nourished and cared for

They are sheltered and protected from harm's way, allowing things to grow to completion

While the Tao creates, it doesn't claim to possess, without taking any credit

Leading by not interfering. This is the way of the Tao

Verse Fifty Two

The Tao which was here before the beginning is considered the mother of all things

Knowing the mother you will know her children. Knowing the children is to embrace the mother. Embracing the mother brings freedom from the fear of death

Go within and guard your outer senses and have everlasting life in peace. Lose your inner self and you'll lose control of your life

The secret of clarity is having the perception of the small. The secret of strength is having the perception of what is soft and tender

He who uses his wisdom of these laws learns to go within himself. Within himself he is safe from harm for he is living in the eternal

For the bright light of the eternal is ever unchanging and free from evil. Learning this principle is to live the Tao

Verse Fifty Three

If I have only the smallest amount of knowledge of the Tao. I will walk the path of the Tao with my only fear being that of straying away

Keeping to the path is easy but people are distracted by the glamour on the side of the path

The royal court is draped in splendor and elegance but the fields lay bare with weeds and the stores are empty, void of provisions for the masses

The court wears elegant clothing carrying sharp swords indulging themselves in food and drink while the poor go unclothed and unfed

They have more possessions than they can use depriving those less fortunate. The ones who boast of this wealth are the thieves and robbers

This is not the way of the Tao

Verse Fifty Four

The Tao is like a tree with deep roots, it is hard to pull up and bring down

The Tao is like what is firmly held in your grasp, it cannot slip away easily. The Tao that is held and practiced will be honored from generation to generation

Learn to cultivate virtue in yourself and virtue will become you. Learn to cultivate virtue in your family and it will grow. Learn to cultivate virtue in the nation and virtue will become abundant. Learn to cultivate virtue in the universe and virtue will be omnipresent

This is the effect of the Tao, from the greatest to the smallest, the Tao is there. As above so below, change the outer by changing the inner, this is the Tao

How do I know the universe behaves this way? By simply looking

Verse Fifty Five

He who is abundantly consumed with virtue is like a newborn child free from the sting of an insect or the fear of an attack from a beast or worried about the claws of birds of prey

Like a newborn child, his bones are soft and his muscles weak but his grasp is strong. The union of man and woman is unknown to him but yet he is complete because he is at his height of vital force

He can cry all day without becoming hoarse as he is in harmony with himself. Experiencing harmony is constancy. Experiencing constancy is enlightenment

It is not wise to rush about from here to there or trying to control the breath as it only causes unnecessary strain. Exhaustion is caused by doing too much

Whoever behaves in this manner will have their years reduced for it is not natural

This is not the way of the Tao

Verse Fifty Six

Those who know do not speak. Those who do speak do not know

He that knows will keep his mouth closed and will keep guard of his senses

Blunt your sharpness, temper your emotions, smooth your rough edges, damper your brightness

Entertain stillness until you become one with the dust of the earth. This is primal union, the mysterious unity

For the Sage that has achieved this state of union is not bothered by profit or lost, kindness or meanness, honor or disgrace, nor does he know the difference between friend or foe

This form of detachment is the highest form for man for he is the noblest one under heaven

Verse Fifty Seven

To be a great leader you must follow the Tao. Wage war only if there are no other options. The world is ruled by non-interference. How do I know this?

By this-

With more laws and regulations the people become poorer. The more weapons a kingdom possesses, the greater the level of strife among the people

With disorder the more disingenuous and corrupt men become, the more strange things take place requiring more laws and regulations hence more thieves and robbers

Therefore the Sage teaches. By practicing non-action the people are reformed. Out of the stillness of peace comes honesty. In doing nothing, the people will prosper by their own hand.

By having no desires the people will return to living a natural life, a life that is simple and good

Verse Fifty Eight

When a country is ruled justly with a light hand the people are simple and good

When a country is ruled with force and a heavy hand, the people become cunning and discontented

Misery is hidden within happiness

Happiness is hidden within misery. Who knows when and how this will end?

When the honest people become dishonest then evil grows for the people are mislead

Therefore the Sage is sharp without cutting in his teachings

Pointed without piercing the people. He is straightforward with being disrupting. And is not blinding with his brilliance

Verse Fifty Nine

It is best to practice moderation and restraint in the governing of people and in the care of nature

Restraint begins with being unselfish and not putting yourself first

Your ability to suceed is based on the virtue that you have stored

If you have accumulated a good store of virtue then nothing is impossible

When nothing is impossible then there are no limits

When a man has no limits, then he is poised to be a great leader

This is from having deep roots and a firm foundation in the way of the Tao

The Tao offers a long fruitful life with inner vision to the eternal

Verse Sixty

Governing a country is like cooking a small fish

Let the country be ruled by the way of the Tao and evil will have no power over the land

It isn't that evil doesn't have power; it is because the way of the Tao protects those who follow it against the way of evil

Like the Sage who harms no one, virtue is allowed to prosper for all the people

Verse Sixty One

A great country is like a stream in the low lands, allowing all to flow to the stream for this becomes the center from which all things in the universe can be ruled, this is the mother of all things

It is in the stillness and quietness that the mother is able to overcome the male

Through this stillness and quietness a great country can overcome a small country

By this principle a small country can overcome a great country

The great suceed by yielding, the small by remaining humble

Verse Sixty Two

The source of the ten thousand things is the Tao. The Tao serves as a treasure for man and as a safe haven for the lost

If someone is lost, offer fine words to awaken him, offer good deeds to him, repay his unkindness with kindness. Do not discard the man but do discard his evil wayward ways

Let your gift to him be living in the way of the Tao

Therefore on the day a leader is elected, do not offer your expertise or wealth to him. Rather help him by staying in the way of the Tao and teach him the way of the Tao. Let your way serve as an example for him to follow

The ancients prized this way in the days of old. It wasn't because the Tao is the source of all good or the cure for evil. But because it is the most noble thing to do thus making it the greatest treasure in the universe

Verse Sixty Three

Practice non-action, work without doing and taste the tasteless. Treat the insignificant with significance; embrace the kind and unkind alike, treating both with the same kindness

See the simplicity in the complicated, see the greatness in the small things and act accordingly

In nature the difficult things are done in an easy manner, great things are made up by the acts of small things; this is the nature of nature, achieving greatness with no effort. This is the law of natural progression

The Sage is like nature in achieving greatness by practicing the law of natural progression in doing small acts to obtain greatness. Promises made without regard to sincerity are often unfulfilled

Treating easy things in life without sincerity often turn them into difficult things. Because the Sage stays on the path of the Tao and practices the laws of nature by approaching all things with sincerity, he never experiences these problems of life

Verse Sixty Four

What resides in stillness is easily managed. Evil can be eliminated before it has formed. The fragile is easily broken. The insignificant can become lost. Confront issues before they become issues

Put things in order before there is disorder. The largest of trees started life as a sapling. A nine story building began with a single brick. A journey of ten thousand miles begins with a single step. By acting it is destroyed, by grasping, it is lost

The Sage doesn't act therefore is not defeated, by not grasping, he doesn't lose

People fail often nearing the end; as much care is needed at the end as it is in the beginning. By giving careful thought from beginning to end, failure is prevented

The Sage has no desires or ambitions for those things difficult, he is detached from precious things and holds on to no ideas

He brings men who are lost back to the way of the Tao, he assists the ten thousand things in their natural progression and he does this by non-interference

Verse Sixty Five

In the days of old, the ancients that followed the Tao did not try to enlighten the masses but kept them in ignorance for it was easier to rule with the people who were simple

The more the people know the harder it is to govern them because of their cleverness. Hence when the king tries to rule with cleverness the country is brought into misfortune

A country that is not ruled by cleverness is brought into good fortune and the land is blessed for the people are simple

The ability to know these two ways of governing and choosing to rule without cleverness is to know the mystic virtue

The mystic virtue is deep rooted and far reaching. It brings all things back into harmony leading them to unity and to the great oneness of the universe

Verse Sixty Six

The great sea is the King to all the streams and rivers of the world. All streams and rivers flow into the great sea. His kingdom is given its power by being below them all

So is the way of the Sage, leading by being behind, by serving in a humble manner

In this approach the people are not threatened or feel oppressed by him. By ruling as a servant the people choose to have him as their king. By this way the people never grow tired of the Sage knowing that no harm can come to them

Because he doesn't compete, there is no competition to meet

Verse Sixty Seven

Everyone in the world talks about my Tao with such familiarity as to its greatness. Because of its greatness it is different from all other teachings thus making it look like a folly

The Tao is not something to be bought or sold at the marketplace, or something that can be put into a box and given away. If this was so then the Tao would have been lost and forgotten years ago. There are three treasures that I hold and keep

The first is unconditional love, the second is frugality; the third is one not putting oneself ahead of others

From unconditional love comes courage. From frugality comes generosity. From not putting oneself ahead of others come leadership

Courage without unconditional love, generosity without frugality, forcing oneself upon people will end in failure

In battle unconditional love will be victorious and will firmly hold its ground. By this very act of unconditional love the heavens will guard those and grant protection to them

Verse Sixty Eight

A good soldier is not prone to violence

A good fighter is not prone to rage

A good winner is not boastful of his victory

A good employer is humble in serving his employees

This is the embodiment of virtue

It is the way of non-striving, non-competing, and being humble.

Being a master of these traits is to know how to use your fellow man to the best of his abilities, allowing him to shine brightly

This has been known since the days of old as a unity of heaven and earth

Verse Sixty Nine

The masters of war have a saying

"I do not dare to be the host; rather I wish to be the guest

I do not dare advance an inch, rather I wish to retreat a foot"

This is called marching with the appearance of not moving, rolling up a sleeve without showing an arm, conquering the enemy without attacking. Being armed without weapons

The greatest disaster in war is underestimating the enemy

Underestimating the enemy can cost you your treasures

And cost you those things that are dearest to you

In battle the victory will go to the one who is the most compassionate

Verse Seventy

My words are easy to know and easy to practice yet few men on earth know of these words and even less are practicing these words

My words are from the times of the ancients, my deeds have a Prince.

Since no one knows this, I am to remain unknown. Those who do know me are few and far in between

And those who do know me should be respected. Knowing me is like having the treasure of jade

Therefore the Sage walks among men with the treasure of jade kept hidden within himself

He covers his body with the rags of a beggar in order to hide the treasure. This the way of the Sage

Verse Seventy One

Having an awareness of ignorance is to know strength

Casting aside ignorance is a disease

Only when we realize that we are riddled with disease do we know that we are sick

Once we become sick of being sick will we be able to move towards health

The Sage is always in a state of health.

His secret is that he chooses health not disease or sickness

Verse Seventy Two

When men no longer have a sense of awe, disaster will follow

Men will begin to look outward from themselves for guidance

For they will no longer trust themselves

In this guidance they will be led astray by a clever ruler

Therefore the Sage doesn't enter their homes and he doesn't interfere with their work

The Sage chooses non-interference so the people will not be confused. He doesn't bring attention to himself rather keeping his self-respect without showing arrogance.

In not exalting himself the Sage chooses to let go of that which he has no need of

Verse Seventy Three

A man of bravery and passion acting without the Tao will be killed or will kill

A man of bravery and calmness acting with the Tao will always preserve life. Of which of these two men is in grace and which is lost? Not all things on earth are favored by heaven. Why is this so? Even the Sage doesn't know all the answers under heaven

Heaven is always at ease, succeeding by not striving. By not striving it overcomes

It doesn't speak yet it is answered. It comes without being called. It achieves its goals without effort. It doesn't ask yet all is provided. Seemly still it moves with ease.

Heavens net covers the universe, while the net is coarse and wide, nothing slips through

Verse Seventy Four

When you realize that all things are constantly changing then you surrender to trying to hold on to anything

When you realize that death is nothing more than an illusion then your fear of death disappears

Men who live in fear of death are afraid of breaking the laws that result in death. Who would dare break such a law that results in death?

There is an official executioner that is responsible for death. Choosing to take his position is like a novice of carpentry trying to work wood like the master carpenter, harm will come to your hand by not knowing the use of the tools.

Verse Seventy Five

When the government taxes are too high, people will go hungry

When the government invades the lives of the people, the people will lose their spirit

Therefore act in the best interest of the people

Trust them and leave them alone

Verse Seventy Six

When a man is born he is soft, gentle and weak. Upon his death he has become hard and stiff

Green plants are the same as man, when young they are supple and tender. At their death they are dry and withered.

Therefore the path of death is unyielding, hard, and stiff whereas the path of life is flexible, soft and supple.

An army that is unyielding and unable to be flexible is assured to be defeated

The hard and unyielding will be defeated

The soft and flexible will succeed

Verse Seventy Seven

The way of the Tao of heaven is like drawing back a bow. The top is brought down while the bottom is brought up. Like the Tao, the bow takes what is abundant and gives to where there is a need. This way the bow maintains balance and harmony.

This is the way the Tao behaves throughout the universe. Keeping balance and harmony by taking from an overabundance and giving to where there is a deficiency. Only the Sage acts in accordance with this law for the ways of man are different.

The way of man is to take from those who don't have enough to give without having regard to their well-being. He uses force to control his fellow man. Desires keep men discontented and in want of more. Rampant ambitions rule their decisions in order to feed their greed. Who can go against this way and instead share his abundance with the world? Only a man that follows the way of the Tao can perform these feats.

Therefore the Sage gives without needing recognition, serves without bringing attention to his actions, he achieves without the need of reward. Once his work is accomplished he moves on. He shows no desire except to help others for this is his wisdom.

Verse Seventy Eight

There is nothing in the world that is weaker or softer than water and yet when it attacks things that are strong and hard, there isn't anything better or more effective than water to create change. It is the weakness that gives water its strength.

The soft can overcome the hard; the gentle can overcome the harsh. While men know this law, very few practice it.

Therefore the Sage says:

Only the one that can carry the burden of men, to take their shame upon himself is worthy to lead his fellow countrymen. Living in serenity amongst the sorrow, free from the evil that abounds, only he can lead the people in a just manner.

The truth often seems paradoxical.

Verse Seventy Nine

When a settlement is reached between two parties where there is great animosity there is bound to be a bitter grudge held by the party that felt he was wronged. How can these thoughts be of benefit to the other?

Therefore the Sage knowing of the bitter grudge will keep the left hand side of the agreement, making no claim on anyone, and will not request a fast settlement from the other party.

He will repay unkindness with kindness for this is the way to end the hostility. For the Sage is with virtue. A man of virtue gives while a man absent of virtue takes.

The way of the Tao is impartial and while impartial the Tao favors the just and kind.

Verse Eighty

When a country is governed with the Tao the citizens are contented

They enjoy the fruit of their labor without the need of machines to save time.

Their love for their home is so deep that they do not desire to travel. While there are carts and boats, they go nowhere. They may have weapons stored but there is no use for them.

They are a happy and simple group that enjoys their food and families ensuring that the needs of the neighborhood are cared for. Their clothing and homes are simple and they live in peace.

Even though they are so close to their neighboring country that the barking of dogs and the crowing of the cocks can be heard, they still have no desire to go, rather staying content to die in their homes of old age having lived a life in peace, love and happiness.

Verse Eighty One

Truthful words are not always beautiful

Beautiful words are not always true

The wise do not argue to prove a point. The men that argue their point are not wise

The Sage doesn't seek to acquire for himself, rather he desires to give to others

The more he gives, the more he has. With this he continues to give more only to receive more.

The way of the Tao is to be giving and not harm

The Sage gives without striving; working without effort, thinking only of others

This is the way of the Tao.

ABOUT THE AUTHOR

Dennis M Waller is recognized as an expert on spiritual experience, self-discovery, and exploring the human consciousness. As writer, speaker and philosopher, his teachings invoke an introspective view on how to discover one's true authentic self through a higher sense of consciousness and awareness. He is best known for his work in the field of Indigos, people who possess unusual or supernatural abilities. His other fields of expertise include comparative religion, the law of attraction, and interpreting Eastern thought's relevancy to science and quantum physics. He is in demand as a guest speaker on radio programs, a lecturer at churches and life enrichment groups, and conducts workshops for Indigos.

Dennis M Waller is the author of "Are You an Indigo, Discover Your Authentic Self" and "The Art of Talking to Christ, The Theory and Practice of Christian Mysticism" and Co-author of "Indigo Wisdom, A Practical Guide to Living a Virtuous Life"

dennismwaller@yahoo.com

www.areyouanindigo.com

Books by Dennis Waller

Zen and Tao, A Little Book on Buddhist Thought

Hsin Hsin Ming

Are You an Indigo? Discover Your Authentic Self

The Art of Talking to Christ

The Tao of Kenny Loggins

Indigo Wisdom with Francesca Rivera

Tao Te Ching- A Translation

Nagarjuna's Tree of Wisdom

Please go to
www.amazon.com/DennisWaller/e/B009HBKD8M
for a complete list of books & audio books

Printed in Great Britain
by Amazon.co.uk, Ltd.,
Marston Gate.